An Aero-Leg...

MW01526926

# Violation

## Violation

**REVOKED**

# FAA ENFORCEMENT ACTIONS

## By Howard J. Fried

# An Aero-Legal Resource Guide

# Violation

## Violation

DEPARTMENT OF TRANSPORTATION FEDERAL AVIATION ADMINISTRATION

**TEMPORARY AIRMAN CERTIFICATE**

CERTIFICATE NO. 000000000

THIS CERTIFIES THAT
iv. John Doe
v. 123 Main Street
Anytown, USA

| DATE OF BIRTH | HEIGHT IN. | WEIGHT | HAIR | EYES | SEX | NATIONALITY | VI. |
|---|---|---|---|---|---|---|---|
| 01-01-75 | | 185 | Brown | Blue | M | USA | |

ix. has been found to be properly qualified and is hereby authorized in accordance with the conditions of issuance on the reverse of this certificate to exercise the privileges of

**Private Pilot**

RATINGS AND LIMITATIONS
xii. Airplane - Single Engine Land

xiii.
THIS IS ☒ AN ORIGINAL ISSUANCE ☐ A REISSUANCE OF DATE OF SUPERSEDED AIRMAN
GRADE OF CERTIFICATE

BY DIRECTION OF THE ADMINISTRATOR

| X. DATE OF ISSUANCE | X. SIGNATURE OF EXAMINER OR INSPECTOR |
|---|---|
| 01-01-93 | *Bill Smith* |

FAA Form 8060-4 (8-79) USE PREVIOUS EDITION

vii. AIRMAN'S SIGNATURE *John Doe*

**REVOKED**

# FAA ENFORCEMENT ACTIONS

**Kindred Spirit Press**

P.O. Box 9132 • Winter Haven, FL 33883-9132 • (941) 294-6396 • Fax (941) 294-3678 • Web Address http://www.kindredsprirt.com

Library of Congress Catalog Card Number 99-63049

ISBN 1-886743-11-8

Printed in the United States of America

10 9 8 7 6 5 4 3 2 1

Cover by: Elizabeth Tolle, Francisco Del Toro Rios Jr.
Graphics by: Elizabeth Tolle
Editors: Amy Sumerlin, Jim Campbell, Howard Fried

Published by:
Kindred Spirit Press, Inc.
P.O. Box 9132
Winter Haven, FL 33883-9132

## Acknowledgments

*Gordon R. Wyllie, a lawyer and a pilot very graciously proofread the manuscript and made several valid suggestions.*

*Jack DiFillippi, a professional artist did a magnificent job on the illustrations. Thanks, Jack!*

*Much of the material in Part 2 of this work previously appeared in* **US Aviator** *magazine and on* **AVWEB**, *the weekly aviation news bulletin on the internet.*

# Contents

## Part 1
## BUSTED!

The Violation Procedure
>The Letter of investigation
>The Notice of Proposed Certificate Action
>The Informal Meeting
>The ASRS Report
>The ALJ Hearing
>The NTSB Hearing and Emergency Revocation

## Part 2
## HORROR  STORIES

A Couple of Horror Stories

>"I'm Going to Get Fried!"

>"I'm Not Interested in Safety"

# Part 3
# SUCCESS!

# Part 4
# DECISIONS AND OPINIONS

# Part 5
# PROTECTION AND DEFENSE

# Part 6
## WHAT TO DO

# *Dedication*

*I used to tell anyone who would listen that I was the happiest guy they were ever going to know, because I was very happily married and I was doing exactly what I wanted to do for a living. That's no longer true. My dear wife of thirty-eight years died while I was working on this book. We had thirty-eight good years together, and unless one has experienced this kind of loss, the effect it has on one can't be appreciated. God, how I miss her! Throughout the writing and publication of my previous books, Myrel offered encouragement and assistance. Therefore, this work is humbly dedicated to Myrel P. Fried.*

*I'm still doing exactly what I love best for a living, and although I'm getting old, I am as retired as I ever intend to be. I go to work almost every day, and I truly enjoy my work. Although I have several other titles, if anyone asks me what I do, I proudly proclaim, "I'm a flight instructor!"*

*I enjoy teaching, and there's nothing that I know of that one can teach in which he or she gets as dramatic a demonstration of the results of his effort as flying. When you help a student, particularly a primary student, over one of those classic learning plateaus, you can see him light up, "Look, it works!" he says. I really get my kicks from this. I fully intend to keep doing this until I am no longer physically able to do so.*

*Howard J. Fried, January, 1999*

# Preface

It has often been said that the problems between the users of the airspace and the Flight Standards Division of the FAA are the result of a few "bad apples" at the bottom level of the agency. I'm here to tell you that that just isn't so. There are not a few bad apples; there are a lot of them. And they are not just at the bottom level. The rot extends all the way to the top.

My experience has shown that there are three kinds of people who populate the Flight Standards District Offices. First, there is a substantial amount of power-mad individuals who delight in harassing (and worse) the users of the airspace. I had to deal with one of these vicious people for several years, and, as you will see, Mike Taylor was victimized by just such a person. These people delight in making life as difficult as possible for those whom they are supposed to assist. Then there is the majority in the middle who are just marking time until they can draw their pensions. These people merely show up for work and do only what is absolutely required, following the dictates of the manual by which their lives are governed. Their main concern is to not rock the boat until they can retire and claim their pensions. This, of course, is typical of the government bureaucracy. Finally, there are the few who are really public servants in the highest sense. These are the ones who go the extra distance to do an outstanding job of helping the airman and the operator to eke out an existence while remaining in compliance with all the burdensome regulations under which they must operate.

As a pilot and the operator of an FAR Part 141 Approved Flight School and an FAR Part 135 On-demand Charter operation, I have encountered all three of these kinds of FAA Inspectors. I had one Principal Inspector charged with supervising my activities whose sole purpose seemed to be to attempt to put me out of business. He did everything possible in his attempt to shut me down. His theory of safety seemed to be that since a pilot is involved in every aircraft accident, ground all the pilots. I've had three of them who did a perfunctory job of supervision, who did the absolute minimum required by their manual. And I've had two who did everything possible to be helpful. One of these two would come out on a Saturday or Sunday to provide a service. The other, knowing that I was conscientiously attempting to remain in full compliance with all the regulations, would help me correct any minor discrepancies he found, rather than writing them up and charging the company with a violation. He would also provide me with helpful information as to how to accomplish various objectives. For these people I am extremely grateful. Their names are Alfred M. Hunt and Neil Humphrey. Al would always go the extra distance to serve the flying public, and Neil was literally a walking regulation book. He knew the regs inside out and he applied them with good judgment and a dry sense of humor. There are also a few guys like Buz Massengale, the Safety Program Manager at the Jackson, MS, FSDO who runs a safety forum every week on America on Line. He, too, goes the extra distance.

Throughout this work I have attempted to maintain the conversational style of writing that my readers tell me they like, but when quoting judges and the National Transportation Safety Board opinions, I, of course, had to use their wording. And this is flowery language indeed. All these legal types seem to think their opinions will carry more weight if they are expressed in two-bit words. They never use a simple, clear word when a long, obtuse one will suffice.

# *Introduction*

The Lawyer Pilots Bar Association Journal, Spring, 1991 issue, reprinted an article by Gary Kwapisz that first appeared in **Aviation Consumer.** Here, he says, "....we do know that people have been driven out of aviation, bankrupted and publicly humiliated by capricious, wrong-headed and incredibly time-consuming FAA enforcement action. Any pilot unfortunate enough to be cited for a violation and thus swept up in the FAA enforcement labyrinth-- whether justifiably so or not--had better know the rules of the FAA's rather complex game. I know of no better way of expressing the literally unbelievable actions of the agency except to add the fact that their rules are subject to change without notice, and change in midstream, right in the middle of an enforcement action. It really takes fancy footwork to follow the maneuvering of some of the agency people involved."

Every law student learns early on that there is absolutely no relationship between the law and justice, between the law and fair play. The FAA has assumed unto itself in matters of discretion its discretion is absolute and that there is no such thing as abuse of discretion. And now the National Transportation Safety Board (NTSB) has affirmed this concept. Writing in the **Journal of the Lawyer Pilots Bar Association** (Winter, 1997 issue), John Yodice points out that "the board will not entertain the defense of selective prosecution." He cites the case of *Administrator v. McCukkough*, NTSB Order No. EA-4592, September 15, 1997, in which the Board stated, "we have no authority to consider issues of selective prosecution by the Administrator." Yodice says, "The Board considers that to be a matter of prosecutorial discretion."

What this tells us is that if an individual Aviation Safety Inspector selects an airman to victimize, the Board will do nothing to stop him. The Taylor case is a perfect case on point. Mike Taylor sent me a copy of a letter he wrote to the FAA Western Regional Manager and asked me to comment on it. This letter, along with my response, is reprinted in its entirety in the appendix. Read it carefully.

On the subject of people, it seems that the FAA, like some law enforcement agencies, manages to attract some power-mad, sadistic individuals who revel in tormenting poor, unfortunate pilots. I actually heard one say, "I love to handle enforcement actions!"

And another (whose official title is "Aviation Safety Inspector") is quoted as saying, "I'm not concerned with Safety. That's the job of the National Transportation Safety Board. My job is to find violations, and that's just what I do!"

This book has been written in an effort to help educate the aviation community regarding the enforcement process and how best to deal with it. Of course, the best way to avoid being caught up in this process is to always operate in full compliance with all the regulations. However, there are two things wrong with this approach. One, an airperson need not actually commit a violation to be charged with doing so; two, it is almost impossible to make a flight without violating one or another of the hodge-podge of rules promulgated by the FAA. Add to this the fact that a great many minor violations occur without the airman being aware of the fact that he or she actually did something contrary to the regulations, and the stage is set for an enforcement action against an individual who is totally unaware of having done anything wrong.

In such cases, the first the airperson knows that he or she is exposed to a sanction (revocation or suspension of his or her pilot certificate or a civil penalty -- fine) is when a Letter of Investigation is received. By that time, it may very well be too late to protect oneself.

If horror stories frighten you, stop now and give this book away. However, if your emotional health can stand it and you would like to know more about the system and how it works, read on.

The term "aviation law" in the collective mind of the public means negligence law and has to do with settlements, suits, and judgments following a major disaster. However, to those who hold airman certificates (pilots, mechanics, repairmen, etc.), "aviation law" is likely to have an entirely different connotation. To these people, it may very well refer to the law embodied in the Code of Federal Regulations, Title 14, commonly referred to as the Federal Air Regulations. Like the Internal Revenue Regulations, these laws are written by lawyers for lawyers. Thus, they can be quite complex and confusing, even to the trained legal mind, let alone the average airperson.

I have, therefore, set about to explain, in simple, easy-to-understand terms, just what the regulations are and how they are interpreted. For starters, let me say that the easiest way to think about the FARs is to understand the fact that there are two bodies of law in the entire world: those laws that are restrictive in nature and those that are permissive in nature.

Permissive laws are such that if they don't say you can do something, you can't do it. FARs are **not** permissive laws. Restrictive laws set forth those things you may not do. Unless they specifically say you can't do it, do so as you please. That's the kind of law embodied in the FARs. You'll notice they all start out, "No person may....., unless....." and then they go on to specify just what preconditions must be met prior to engaging in whatever activity is contemplated.

Consequently, to avoid violating the regulations, we must know which things are prohibited. That's not always easy. In fact, it is virtually never easy. Many times the regulation writers scatter the elements of a particular activity through several different regulations so they must be cross-referenced to find just what they really say, and this doesn't take into account the matter of interpretation!

This material is organized to first give an overview of the enforcement process, and then to show with case law how the regulations have been interpreted -- first by the FAA, then by an NTSB (National Transportation Safety Board) ALJ (Administrative Law Judge), then by the NTSB itself, and finally in some cases, by the United States Courts, at the level of the Circuit Courts of Appeal, except for the Supreme Court, the highest court in the land.

No matter how narrowly a law is written, it seems that there is always more than one way of interpreting its meaning, and with respect to the FARs, there are usually several different interpretations of any given regulation. It has been said that there are as many FAAs as there are Regional Offices, and clearly there are as many as there are District Offices. It also seems that there really are as many FAAs as there are ASIs (Aviation Safety Inspectors), for each one interprets the regulations as he sees fit. Additionally, since the FAA is characteristically incapable of making a mistake,* whatever interpretation an individual inspector places on a given regulation becomes the law at that time and place. And until the NTSB or a court says differently, the airperson is stuck with the ASI's decision, for the FAA will back up whatever any of its inspectors says. No matter how blatant an error, the FPA (Federal Protective Association) kicks in and closes ranks behind the inspector who made the erroneous pronouncement.

That the whole system is so hidebound by its manuals and procedures as to allow no room for logic and reason is amply illustrated by the following two true stories:

Several years ago I gave a Commercial Practical Test to a Catholic Priest, a popular local aviator called "Father Joe". It was one of those panic situations in which I was called to administer the test that very day (a Sunday), for the good father was scheduled to depart for a mission up the Amazon River the next morning.

Father Joe passed his checkride and when I made out his temporary certificate, I noticed that although his medical and written result stated his name as "Guiseppi Giovano Panizzio", the old Private Pilot Certificate he was turning in showed his name to be "Joseph J. Panizzio". I was well aware that Guiseppi equates with Joseph in Italian, but I told him this could pose a problem.

He explained that when he came to this country he wanted to become Americanized, so he called himself Joseph. However, he later decided that since he had pride in his Italian heritage, he reverted to the original spelling. Not being able to do anything else under the circumstances, I accepted the situation as it existed and sent in the paperwork.

Sure enough, it bounced like a rubber ball. The local FSDO informed me that I would have to get from Father Panizzio a court order changing his name. They said their rules require that if the name on the old certificate is different from that on the written result and the new temporary certificate, they would have to have either a court order confirming a name change (or a copy of a marriage license in the case of a woman who had committed matrimony).

There, of course, was no way of reaching Father Joe, who by this time was off in the jungle someplace. Besides, he didn't have a court order in the first place.

Can you believe it took five months, during which time the temporary certificate expired, to get the FAA to accept things as they were? The local District Office was absolutely adamant in their refusal to forward the paperwork to OKC. Finally, I called the Airman Records Branch myself and got a favorable reply, which ultimately satisfied the guys here, and they went ahead and submitted the file.

The foregoing story illustrates the manner in which the bureaucrats in the FAA are so stuck on their procedures and inflexible in the way they follow them, and so afraid that someone at a higher level will criticize something they do.

Now let me show you how they back up the people who make obvious mistakes. A few years ago my wife, who practiced law and did quite a bit of work opposing the FAA, had a woman client come to her with the following story.

The lady held an ATP Pilot Certificate as well as a CFII. She had not flown for six years. She and her husband owned a Beechcraft Baron and she decided she wanted to fly her own airplane, exercising only Private Pilot privileges. Therefore, she went to an AME (Aviation Medical Examiner) and was examined for and received a Third Class Medical Certificate.

Near the bottom of the application form in use at that time is the question "Have you been hospitalized since your last examination?" If the answer is "Yes," the next question is "If yes, what for?" The lady checked "Yes" and put down two words, "Radical Mastectomy."

When the paperwork arrived at the CAMI (Civil Air Medical Institute) in Oklahoma City, some bottom-line clerk who didn't know what that meant decided it must be bad and denied the medical.

In due course, the lady received by registered mail a letter demanding the submission of her medical certificate. This, she ignored. After several more registered letters, two Federal Marshals showed up on her doorstep and demanded the medical certificate, which, at this time, she surrendered.

She then retained the services of my wife. My wife, being the kind of lawyer who liked to do things the easy way, picked up the phone and called the CAMI. She spoke first to the clerk who had originally denied the medical and then to her supervisor, who, after hearing a complete explanation of the situation said, "Of course the woman should have her medical."

My wife said, "Fine. Send it back."

The response was, "Oh, I can't do that. It would put me in the position of overruling my subordinate."

Two more steps up the line, my wife finally reached the top guy, who, in order to return the certificate, would have had to overrule four people who had already denied the medical.

It took several months and a full NTSB hearing to get the medical back for that lady!

Don't think for a minute that these are extreme examples of the attitude of the bureaucrats in the FAA. They are simply typical of how the agency acts to protect their own no matter how wrong and to follow their procedures no matter how ridiculous. They do, however, tend to demonstrate the absurdity of the system.

The ridiculous extreme to which the FAA will go to enforce its regulations, whether or not they have to do with safety, is well known. And their definition of "airworthy" is something else. In his column "Pilot Counsel" in the AOPA magazine *PILOT*, John Yodice recently cited two cases that illustrate this point.

The first dealt with a FAR Part 135 single engine operator, who in an effort to comply with the regulations, placarded one of the two glide slope receivers in his Cherokee as "inop".

An Aviation Safety Inspector observed this placard and issued a violation of FAR 91.213. You should know that the Cherokee was not required to have a glide slope, and under Part 135, the operator was not allowed to fly IFR. Regardless, the airplane was deemed "unairworthy" because one of the **two** it did have wasn't working!

The other case Yodice cited was even worse in terms of "airworthiness". Delta Airlines was fined $400 because the indicator light on a switch on a piece of galley equipment wasn't working. Please understand that the switch worked fine and it was readily apparent as to whether it was in the "on" or "off" position, but the inoperative indicator light rendered the airplane "unairworthy"!

Do those two situations sound to you as though the respective airplanes were "unairworthy"? Of course not. Not by any definition except that of the FAA.

*Remember the Hoover case? The agency never admitted it was wrong to ground that great airman. Rather, although there was no change whatsoever in his "condition", when the pressure to restore his medical certificate became so great that they had to do something, they solved the problem and attempted to save face by saying, "He got better." What a load of crap! What he really got was three years older, three years during which he was deprived of his livelihood.

*Howard Fried with AOPA's Chief Counsel,
John Yodice*

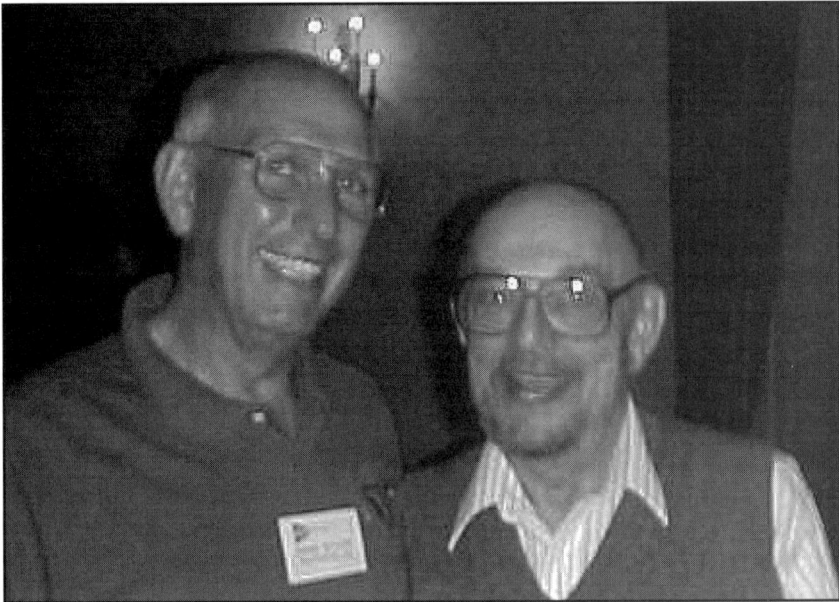

*Author Fried with respected NTSB Law Judge
Roger Mullins*

PART 1
BUSTED!

# Chapter 1

## The Violation Procedure

**" This Airplane is Unairworthy "**

## The Letter of Investigation

Unlike the FAA, I **am** here to help you – by preparing you to deal with the Friendly Feds if and when you are ever confronted with an enforcement action. Many of us who hold airman certificates of one kind or another spend a lifetime without ever having contact with the Flight Standards division of the FAA (knock on wood), but others are not so fortunate. If you have never had the misfortune to experience an enforcement action, listen up. It can happen to you, and it can happen at any time, and it would help you to know what to expect if and when it does.

If an airman inadvertently violates a regulation and is unaware of having done so, the first indication he or she gets that all is not well is the LOI, or Letter of Investigation. It comes by way of registered mail, and it is the aviator's invitation to hang him/herself. The LOI is cleverly worded so as to appear to require an answer, but it is not mandatory that an answer be offered. It goes like this:

*It has come to the attention of this office that a violation of....(section number).... of the Federal Aviation Regulations may have occurred on....(date).... at....(location).... and we have reason to believe you may have been involved. We would appreciate receiving any evidence or statements you might care to make regarding this matter. Any discussion or written statements made by you will be given consideration in our investigation. You have ten days to respond to this letter of investigation or we will be forced to proceed without benefit of hearing your side of the story.*

Sounds like you'd better rush right out and reply before the ten days runs out, doesn't it? Not so! You are under no compulsion to do so, and many attorneys advise airpersons not to answer at all. I believe this is a mistake. The first step you should take after receiving a LOI is to retain the services of a knowledgeable attorney, unless you are prepared to do extensive research, in which case you may represent yourself (see Chapter 3). Then ask him/her to answer the LOI, but say nothing. Nobody likes to be ignored, so the thing to do is address the investigating inspector by name and say, "Thank you for giving me (or my client) the opportunity to respond, but I do not wish to make a statement at this time."

You should also know that the phrase, "Any discussion or written statements made by you will be given consideration in our investigation" simply means that the Friendly Feds will consider anything you say in the worst possible light and use it against you. That's what they mean by "giving consideration." They are simply offering you an opportunity to say something they can use against you.

Of course, if you were in Europe at the time of the alleged violation, and it occurred in Ohio, you should answer the LOI with a statement to that effect. Or if the LOI specifies the tail number of your airplane, and it was in pieces on the maintenance hangar floor being worked on at the time of the alleged violation, you should say so. Otherwise say nothing!

Since this is an administrative civil action, the courts have ruled that although there is no warning to that effect, there is no Fifth Amendment protection against self-incrimination. Anything you say can and most certainly will be used against you in any subsequent action, resulting in the suspension, or worse, the revocation of your certificate.

Depending on which form of the LOI you receive, it may suggest the possibility of remedial training in lieu of certificate action. Beware! Unless you meet certain very specific criteria, you won't be eligible for remedial training. If you spill your guts and it turns out you are not eligible for this alternative to certificate action, whatever you say can -- and no doubt will -- be used to convict you of the violation, and certificate action will surely result. The LOI, the form that mentions remedial training, does not tell you just what requirements you must meet to be eligible.

These requirements are:
1. The violation must be inadvertent rather than deliberate.
2. It must not be in a commercial operation as opposed to personal pleasure or business.
3. It should, but does not have to be, a first offense.
4. You can't have previously benefited from remedial training in lieu of certificate action on a previous offense.
5. No accident or injury resulted from the violation.
6. You display a cooperative attitude.

If any one or more of these conditions exist, or fail to exist, you will not be eligible for remedial training. If you say anything at all, you will only find yourself in deeper trouble, so once again it is best to say nothing, particularly anything that can be used against you. If you do, you will surely be hit with it in whatever action the FAA decides to take against you.

The next step in the process is another registered letter stating the result of the investigation and informing you that a finding of violation has been made. This letter is entitled NOTICE OF PROPOSED CERTIFICATE ACTION. It cites the specific regulation or regulations that are alleged to have been violated and the specific actions that constituted the violations, along with the date and location of the occurrence.

### The Notice of Proposed Certificate Action (1)

The next step in the violation process after the airperson

receives the Letter of Investigation (LOI) and either answers or doesn't answer, is almost certain to be a NOTICE OF PROPOSED CERTIFICATE ACTION. This, which also comes by way of certified mail, states the penalty the FAA intends to impose on the alleged violator. It concludes by offering the airman five choices. (Just check the appropriate box and return the letter to the Office of the Regional Counsel.) Sure you will!

This letter says:
*In reply to your Notice of Proposed Certificate Action...., I elect to proceed as indicated below:*

*1. I hereby transmit my certificate with the understanding that an Order will be issued as proposed effective the date of mailing of this reply.*

*2. I request that the order be issued so that I may appeal directly to the National Transportation Safety Board.*

*3. I hereby submit my answer to your Notice and request that my answer and any information attached thereto be considered in connection with the allegations set forth in your Notice.*

*4. I hereby request to discuss this matter informally with an attorney at the Office of the Regional Counsel....*

*5. I hereby submit evidence of the timely filing of an Aviation Safety Report with NASA concerning the incident set forth in the Notice of Proposed Certificate Action and thereby claim entitlement to waiver of any penalty.*

Let us briefly consider each of these choices:
Almost nobody checks the first box and surrenders his or her certificate. If this choice is selected, the clock starts running on the

suspension and the airperson is grounded for whatever period of time the FAA has demanded. The airperson has given up without a fight, without even a mild objection.

Some aviation attorneys have their clients select choice number two and go directly to a hearing before a NTSB Administrative Law Judge. They feel that the intervening steps are wastes of time. Until the hearing, the airperson keeps his certificate and continues to exercise its privileges.

Choice number three, submitting a written account of the airperson's side of the story, merely exposes his defenses to the other side and is rarely a wise move. The FAA almost never pays any attention to whatever excuse the airman offers. It also gives the airperson another opportunity to say something that can be used against him or her.

The majority of airmen (and the term includes women as well as men) opt for choice number four, which results in a hearing before an NTSB Administrative Law Judge, an ALJ.

If choice number four is selected, the next step in the process after the alleged violator receives the Notice of Proposed Certificate Action is likely to be what is called an informal hearing, since this is what most airpersons and aviation attorneys request. This really is a meeting with the investigating Inspector from the District Office, an associate counsel (lawyer) from the Regional Office of the FAA, and the alleged violator, who may or may not be accompanied by his attorney. Per our previous discussion of the LOI, the airperson should certainly have his lawyer with him. I know of at least one case in which the informal meeting was conducted by telephone between the investigating inspector, an FAA associate counsel, and the airman's lawyer. The airman himself wasn't even notified of the meeting. But as I mentioned above, the airman is usually there.

It is at this point that the gloves come off, and all pretense of cooperation on the part of the FAA goes out the window and a purely adversarial situation arises. The FAA attorney plays both prosecutor and judge. The investigating Aviation Safety Inspector plays witness for the prosecution, and the airperson plays victim. In many cases the FAA attorney (from the Office of the Associate General Counsel, formerly the Office of the Regional Counsel) has no authority to do anything but inform the alleged violator as to what sanction (penalty) will be imposed. In these cases, literally anyone capable of acting as a messenger could convey the proposed penalty to the airman and his or her attorney. They don't need a lawyer for this.

In other cases the FAA attorney may be in a position to compromise the penalty and the airman may wind up with a lesser sanction than was originally demanded by the Friendly Feds, although this is extremely unlikely. In those cases where a compromise does occur, it is usually a situation in which the FAA gives up something they never intended to get in the first case. It is not unlike the games they play with NPRMs (Notices of Proposed Rule Making). Have you noticed how some of the stuff in most NPRMs is so outrageous that it is dropped, supposedly in response to the responses received? This is stuff they never intended to get in the first place, but when it is dropped from the Final Rule it gives the FAA an opportunity to look like good guys.

After a full discussion of all the facts surrounding the alleged violation, the FAA attorney may close the matter with a finding of no violation (again, extremely unlikely), modify the penalty (sanction) by, for example, knocking down a proposed 60-day suspension of the airman's certificate to 30 days (very unlikely), or affirm the sanction as proposed (quite likely). He or she might even attempt to increase the sanction. However, as mentioned above, in some instances he has no authority to do anything. He is sent from the regional office with instructions to impose the proposed penalty and that's all he can do. There is an advantage to opting to have one of these informal meetings. It gives the airman and his lawyer an opportunity to see just what evidence the government has against the alleged violator. The lawyers spar around, each trying to find out as much as he can about the other's case.

Whatever the outcome of this informal meeting, the airman may appeal to the NTSB, just as if s/he had chosen option number two in the Notice of Proposed Certificate Action. At this point, a hearing before an ALJ is scheduled. It is not really scheduled in terms of a specific date, but it is put on the agenda. Some time in the future (quite a long time) a date for the hearing is set. At this hearing sworn testimony is taken, and a record is made (court reporter and all). This hearing before the Administrative Law Judge comes next in the process.

As far as choice number five is concerned, if the airman has, within ten days of the occurrence, submitted an Aviation Safety Reporting System report to the National Aeronautics and Space Administration, an ASRS, or as it is called, a NASA report, he may check choice number five. If an airperson is ever involved in an incident that may or may not include a violation on his part, he may be able to obtain partial protection by filing one of these ASRS reports. The program was initiated in 1975 and its objective is to gather information to help make the system safer for all of us. In an effort to gather information and compile statistics to help plan a safer aviation system in the United States, persons holding airman certificates (pilots and mechanics), have been granted limited immunity from sanctions, or penalties. NASA has been given control of this system so it is completely separate and apart from the FAA, the bad guys who are out to get the certificate holder.

It works like this: If within ten days of the occurrence, the airperson files a report with NASA explaining what happened, and he or she is subsequently charged with a regulation violation by the FAA, he is immune from the penalty that would normally result from the violation. Please understand, the violation remains on the airman's record; s/he just doesn't suffer the penalty. The report is sent to NASA at Moffett Field in California and given a number to protect the anonymity of the airman. A receipt, which is mailed back to the reporter, serves to prove that the report was filed timely (within the ten-day limit) and may be used to enable the airman to escape whatever sanction the FAA might be seeking to impose. This immunity from sanction is severely limited by several qualifying criteria, such as the violation must have been inadvertent as opposed to deliberate. By the bye, here's another example of the arrogant way in which the FAA itself disregards the regulations. When an airperson avails him or herself of immunity by timely filing an ASRS Report, the record of violation is supposed to be expunged after a period of time, but there are numerous recorded instances where this was not done. Most Air Carrier pilots and many General Aviation pilots carry a supply of these NASA reporting forms in their flight bags, and they submit a report every time there is even a hint that a violation might be forthcoming.

NASA publishes a summary of these ASRS reports monthly in newsletter form entitled **Callback**. It is distributed free to anyone requesting to be put on the mailing list. If you want to learn from the adventures, misadventures, and mistakes of others, it is well worth reading. Everyone who holds an airman certificate of any kind should be on the mailing list for **Callback** and should spend a few minutes each month reading and analyzing these summaries. The address is: National Aeronautics and Space Administration, Ames Research Center, Moffett Field, CA 94036-1000.

### The Hearing Before the NTSB ALJ

Following the preliminaries, the Letter of Investigation, the Notice of Proposed Certificate Action, and the informal hearing (meeting), the next step in processing an alleged violation of the regulations is a formal hearing before a NTSB Administrative Law Judge (ALJ). Often this step follows the Notice of Proposed Certificate Action without an intervening informal hearing (meeting) with an FAA attorney from the regional office. Many lawyers who make a practice of representing clients accused of violating the regulations feel that the informal is a waste of time and check choice number two on the Notice of Proposed Certificate Action. They go directly to a hearing before an NTSB ALJ. There is always quite a long wait for this hearing (usually several months). The ALJ, in addition to hearing other transportation-type cases, is responsible for a great many District Offices of the FAA, and he can only get around to each of them infrequently. When he does come into a district, he hears several violation cases during the few days he spends there. There is an exception to this. When the FAA exercises its emergency revocation authority, the wait for a hearing is quite brief, but that's another story.

The burden of proof here is on the government, just as in a criminal trial, but the standard is quite different, because it is considered a civil matter. Instead of having to prove its case "beyond a reasonable doubt" as in a criminal trial, the government needs only to meet the standard of a "preponderance of the evidence". As you can imagine, some ALJs are inclined to weigh the testimony of the FAA Inspector more heavily than that of the other witnesses.

At this point, the proceedings become quite formal. The Associate General Counsel, who had conducted the informal, if there was one, acts as prosecutor. Although other witnesses may be called, the Aviation Safety Inspector from the District Office who conducted the investigation and gathered the facts surrounding the incident is the main witness for the prosecution. A court reporter is present and makes a record of the testimony. Both parties (the Government and the alleged violator) have subpoena power to compel the presence of witnesses. This hearing has all the trappings of a criminal trial, except the accused has none of the constitutional protections of a criminal defendant. You should also know that by this time the procedure will become quite expensive, with attorney fees, and other costs, plus the time off work that it takes to defend oneself.

The ALJ is employed by the NTSB and hears all kinds of transportation cases -- from railroad matters to highway situations as well as aviation cases. During this procedure s/he listens carefully (although I am aware of at least one case in which the ALJ slept quietly throughout the taking of testimony) to all the testimony before rendering a decision, which may or may not affirm the finding of the FAA. He may, and sometimes does, find that either no violation occurred or that the FAA failed to prove its case and the alleged violator is off the hook entirely. You should also know that, no matter what violation or violations allegedly have occurred, the dear old FAA invariably throws in a few more charges to be used as bargaining chips in negotiating with the alleged violator and/or his lawyer.

Frequently, even though the ALJ finds that a violation did indeed occur, and the accused is indeed guilty of having committed the violation, if there are mitigating circumstances, the ALJ will modify the penalty sought by the FAA (knock a sixty-day suspension down to thirty days, for example). ALJs seem to be particularly sensitive to airmen who earn their living as aviators. If the airperson is a professional pilot or mechanic, the ALJ will frequently look for an excuse to avoid depriving him/her of his/her livelihood for any longer than absolutely necessary. As an example, here's an interesting true story:

My wife, an attorney whose practice included a moderate amount of work defending airmen accused of violations, had this one. At the time when a Terminal Control Area violation called for a mandatory sixty-day suspension of a pilot's certificate, a rather prominent pilot took off from Pontiac, Michigan for Atlanta, Georgia at 1:00 a.m. to deliver a load of cargo. His course took him right through the Detroit TCA. He called the appropriate approach controller and announced, "I'm off Pontiac for Atlanta climbing to eight thousand five-hundred VFR." The controller identified him and vectored him right through the TCA, but neglected to use the language "Cleared through the TCA." (The FAA is in love with words, and insists that the correct ones be used). The next day, a supervisor was monitoring the previous night's tape to check on his controller. Not hearing the phrase "cleared through the TCA," he notified Flight Standards and a violation was issued against the pilot for being in the TCA without a clearance. At the informal, the FAA attorney demanded the pilot's certificate for sixty days, and an appeal was taken to the NTSB. The controller testified that he meant to clear the flight through the TCA, but simply neglected to say the word "cleared." The FAA attorney played the tape in the courtroom and said, "I didn't hear anyone say 'Cleared through the TCA.'"

The Administrative Law Judge said, "Well, it's true he was in the TCA without a clearance, but clearly he thought he had a clearance, and the controller thought he had cleared him. However, I can't let him off altogether." And turning to the pilot, he went on, "Your pilot certificate is hereby suspended for a period of ten days. I want you to find a period of ten days within the last two years during which you didn't fly, and that will be your suspension."

The effect of this, of course, was that there was no suspension at all, but the violation still went on the pilot's record and if he's ever involved in another violation it will be a second offense. The FAA attorney wasn't too happy with this outcome, although he did not take an appeal to the full Board.

This factor of taking mitigating circumstances into account is almost never applied by the FAA itself, even back at the informal stage. They almost always go for the most severe penalty they can. It is this implacable attitude on the part of the FAA that has caused the users (airpersons) to distrust the agency. The adversarial position that has grown between the agency and the people with whom it is supposed to work is a direct result of the attitude of many of the agency's employees.

Regardless of the outcome of the NTSB ALJ hearing, both sides have the right of appeal to the full NTSB. If the ALJ finds that the accused did indeed commit a violation but reduces the penalty the FAA is seeking to impose, and the agency feels that the reduction is unjustified, it will likely appeal to the Board itself in an attempt to get the penalty increased.

If, on the other hand, the airperson is found to have been guilty of committing the alleged violation or violations and he or she believes that an error of law has occurred, s/he may appeal to the Board.

### The National Transportation Safety Board Hearing And Emergency Revocation

If an airperson has the financial ability and believes strongly enough in his/her cause, an appeal may be taken from the decision of an NTSB Administrative Law Judge. And if such an appeal is filed, after a wait of several more months, another formal hearing takes place. This time, the whole Board sits in judgment on the matter. The Board may affirm, reverse, or modify the decision of the Administrative Law Judge, and all three results are not uncommon.

This appeal is based on the record made at the NTSB ALJ hearing, but oral argument is usually heard. This hearing is the final step in the administrative law process. Unless constitutional issues are involved, in which case the matter can be moved into the federal law courts at the level of the United States Circuit Court of Appeals, the NTSB hearing is the end of the road. There are no more appeals, and both sides must accept this final judgment. The violation adjudication process is over. Of course an appeal may be taken to the Supreme Court, but this almost never happens. Throughout this entire process, which may last well over a year, the airperson continues to exercise the privileges of his/her certificate unless the FAA utilizes the single exception to this.

Before we get into specific cases, this matter should be addressed. I am referring to the power granted to the FAA to take immediate action to revoke the certificate of a suspected violator without a hearing of any kind if there is an urgent safety reason to do so. This extraordinary power was given to the FAA to prevent the continuation of a dangerous situation and to enable the agency to yank a certificate that was issued in error or as the result of a fraudulent application, false logbook entries or some such thing.

When the FAA exercises its power of emergency revocation, the airperson is effectively and immediately grounded. As a result, he or she is entitled to an immediate hearing before the NTSB so that if no urgent safety reason for revocation is found, the airperson's certificate can be restored without undue delay.

The law requires that there be an imminent danger if the

airperson should be allowed to continue to exercise his/her privileges while the administrative process is pending. The problem here is that the agency will, in its arrogance, abuse this emergency revocation authority. They will frequently yank a certificate when there is no imminent threat to safety. This unwarranted action on the part of the FAA is likely to make the NTSB unhappy, for the Board must adjust its extremely busy schedule and drop its routine matters to hear the emergency case. The Board has consistently urged the agency to use discretion in the exercise of its emergency authority, and the agency has just as consistently ignored the Board in its zeal to go after a particular airperson.

One of the most blatant abuses of power at the hands of the FAA has been its use of this emergency revocation power. The exercise of this technique was designed to prevent the continuation of an unsafe condition or activity, but the agency hasn't hesitated to use it in cases where no emergency whatsoever existed, almost to the extent that it has become routine. Fortunately for the aviation community, an airman who has had his certificate revoked under the emergency authority where no emergency exists -- if he or she is willing to fight the revocation in the courts -- can prevail, and even recoup the costs of the fight.

Until the case of *Daryl R. Frank et al v. James B. Busey, FAA Administrator*, case No. 91-1469 (United States Court of Appeals for the District of Columbia, October, 1991), the NTSB and the courts had been most reluctant to impose any limits on the discretionary powers of the agency. However, in that case, the court determined that since the alleged violations had occurred some eighteen months previously and the investigation had been ongoing for that length of time, there was no immediate danger to safety that would require the emergency revocation of the five pilot certificates in question. The *Frank* case is the first, and so far only, crack in the wall of non-accountability built around the FAA. Until this landmark case, both the NTSB and the courts have refused to put any limit on the discretionary powers of the FAA. Mary Schiavo, former Inspector General for the Department of Transportation says, "The FAA has built a culture of nonaccountability."

We must bear in mind, however, that this decision (*Frank*) has not prevented the agency from continuing to abuse its emergency power to revoke the certificates of airmen when no real emergency exists. It simply means that each case must be fought individually, and if the FAA can demonstrate no genuine emergency involving safety, the airman is likely to prevail. This stubborn refusal of the FAA to relinquish any of the power it has assumed unto itself (without any justification whatever) has forced each individual airperson to fight for his/her rights on an individual basis.

Of course, if and when the airperson prevails, as he or she well may, s/he can recover the costs of the battle under the Equal Access to Justice Act. This is just about the only way in which the agency can be held accountable for the actions of its employees. However, this can be a long and involved process.

Because the FAA has consistently abused its power of emergency revocation and the tremendous amount of adverse publicity resulting from the treatment of R. A. (Bob) Hoover at the hands of the agency, Senator James Inhofe of Oklahoma has, as this is being written, introduced the so-called "Hoover Bill." This bill is designed to force the FAA to demonstrate the urgent need to invoke the emergency revocation power.

Obviously, there is a definite need for the existence of this extraordinary power in legitimate cases, but if passed, this bill would give the airperson forty-eight hours to demand that the FAA prove the nature of the actual emergency.

(1) *If the alleged offense did not occur in actual flight, instead of a Notice of Proposed Certificate Action, the certificate holder receives a Notice of Proposed Civil Penalty, stating the fine the FAA is seeking. The procedure following this notice is the same as that which follows the NOPCA (informal, ALJ hearing, etc.), except in those cases in which the fine (civil penalty) exceeds $10,000. In this case, the matter is moved over to the Federal Court System instead of being heard by the ALJ and the NTSB.*

## ENFORCEMENT FLOW CHART

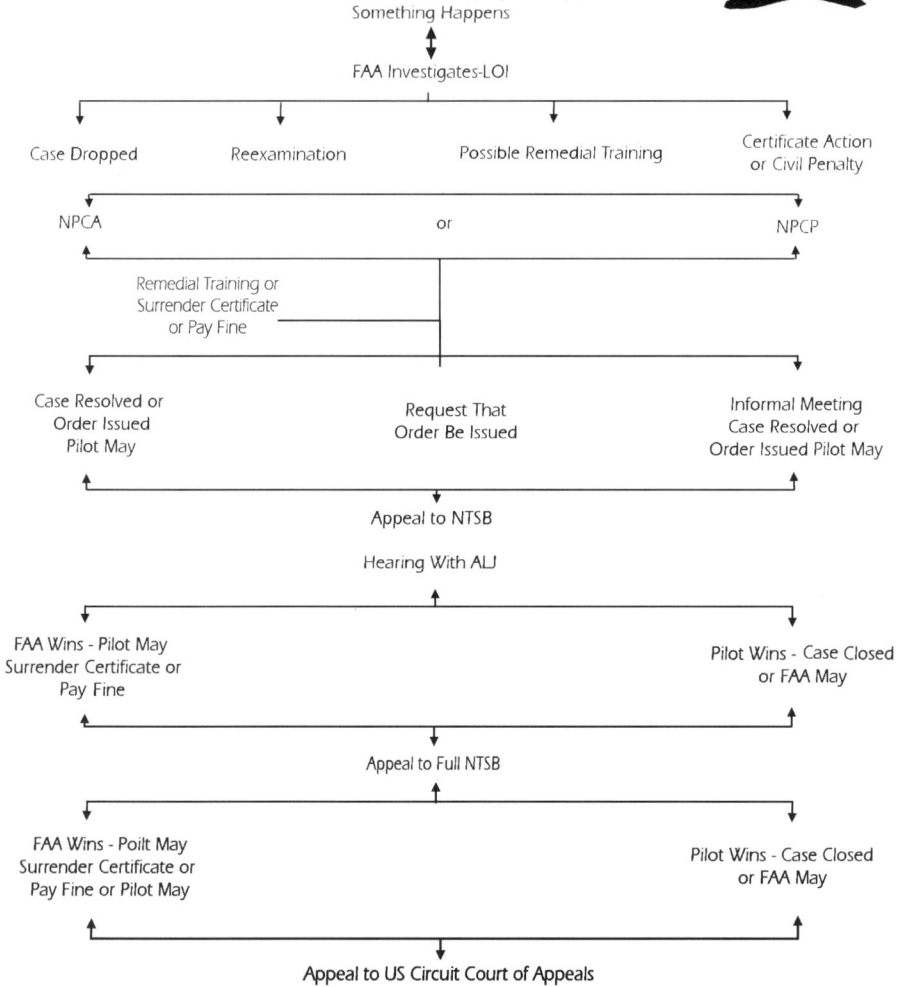

Something Happens

FAA Investigates-LOI

| Case Dropped | Reexamination | Possible Remedial Training | Certificate Action or Civil Penalty |

NPCA      or      NPCP

Remedial Training or
Surrender Certificate
or Pay Fine

| Case Resolved or Order Issued Pilot May | Request That Order Be Issued | Informal Meeting Case Resolved or Order Issued Pilot May |

Appeal to NTSB

Hearing With ALJ

| FAA Wins - Pilot May Surrender Certificate or Pay Fine | | Pilot Wins - Case Closed or FAA May |

Appeal to Full NTSB

| FAA Wins - Poilt May Surrender Certificate or Pay Fine or Pilot May | | Pilot Wins - Case Closed or FAA May |

Appeal to US Circuit Court of Appeals

**PART 2**
**HORROR STORIES**

# Chapter 2
## A Couple of Horror Stories

### "I'm Going to Get Fried!"
### Inspector David Sunday, Detroit FSDO

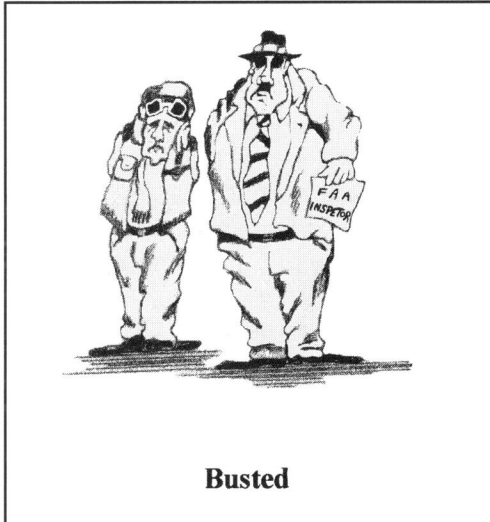

**Busted**

I know I'm no Robert A. (Bob) Hoover, whose troubles with the FAA are well known and in whose case the FAA steadfastly refuses to admit they did anything wrong, but my problems with the agency are at least as bad, or worse, and obviously equally unjust. The Hoover case is an excellent example of the FAA's obstinate refusal to admit to having made a mistake or to admit to any of their employees having done anything wrong. In Hoover's case, after exercising the extraordinary emergency power of revocation to take away his medical and put him through two years of extensive and expensive medical testing, they restored his medical certificate, declaring, "He got better." Actually, all he really got was three years older, during which time he was grounded and deprived of his livelihood. This statement, "He got better" was the FAA response to the public outcry over the outrageous treatment of that great aviator and the FAA's attempt to save face.

In 1972, an inspector from our local District Office of the FAA (Flight Standards District Office--FSDO), David Sunday, told an operator at the airport where I am based, "I'm going to get Fried!" (The operator, a freight hauler, has provided me with a notarized affidavit testifying to this statement). Sunday's opportunity came a few months later when the FAA, in a knee-jerk reaction to an article in the Wall Street Journal criticizing the pilot examiner program, asked each district office to look at the records of their high volume examiners, of which I was one. (I had been conducting over three hundred certification flight tests annually for the past several years.)

After seventeen years as a faithful representative of the Administrator, in May of 1992 I was shocked to be informed that my designation as a Pilot Examiner was not to be renewed. It happened like this: Routinely, more than thirty days prior to the annual expiration of my designation, I had always received the paperwork required for renewal. My anniversary date was in May, and the designation must be renewed before the end of the month, or an examiner must start all over again with attendance at the initial course at Oklahoma City (at his own expense). In 1992 I received no such notification or application, so I called and requested it as well as an appointment for meeting and ride with an inspector for renewal.

I was told that the paperwork would be taken care of when I came in and an appointment was made for me to do so. Over a period of three weeks, I was given three separate appointments, each of which was canceled by the FAA.

The final appointment offered by Inspector Sunday, who was acting for Inspector Scarpuzza, the principal inspector assigned to work with me, was for a day when he knew I could not make it due to a prior commitment. If we didn't get together that day, there was no other time prior to the expiration of my designation. I was, however, able to rearrange my schedule to accommodate Sunday's offered time, so I called him back and agreed to come in at the time he offered me.

Incidentally, I'm convinced that Inspector Scarpuzza

orchestrated the entire attack on me. He merely used Sunday as a stooge to do his dirty work. The previous year at the time of the renewal of my designation, Scarpuzza had taken away my authority to administer practical tests in three make and model twins and in gliders, claiming that an examiner wasn't needed for these airplanes. However, within six weeks, he had conferred that multi-engine authority on another examiner. Shortly after that, a new glider examiner was designated. Obviously there existed a need for an examiner for those three twins and for gliders. Scarpuzza had lied when he advised me to the contrary.

The next day Dave Sunday called and canceled that final appointment, saying I'd be getting a letter of explanation, but refusing to tell me what was in the letter. The following day, both by messenger and by registered mail, I received a letter informing me that my designation was not going to be renewed. The letter advised me that I could come in to the FSDO (with legal counsel if I wished) and appeal this decision. This allowed me one working day in which to be renewed or I would automatically be disqualified. (In the case of a favored examiner, however, many months after his designation had expired, the Detroit FSDO saw fit to "renew" him by retro-dating the paperwork to a date prior to the expiration of his designation, thus avoiding the necessity of him having to travel to Oklahoma City and attend the original examiner course.) Can you believe the arrogance of these people? They do whatever they wish with a total disregard of their own rules.

Immediately after I received the letter denying my renewal, a half-dozen local attorneys offered to accompany me to an appeal meeting at the FSDO the following day (the last working day prior to automatic disqualification). I selected one and we went to the District Office together. The first thing we were told was that I was entitled to due process and specifically "adequate notice". I looked across the table to the Office Manager and asked, "Dave (Hobgood), do you *really* believe **one day** is adequate notice?"

He smiled (smirked), and said, "Of course it is!"

This set the tone for the balance of the meeting. My attorney suggested that my designation be renewed pending the outcome of an official appeal. This request was denied out of hand, and the appeal process was explained to us. We were also presented with a memo explaining the appeal process, which starts at the District

Office, and from which an appeal may be made to the Regional Office (of the FAA). Finally, the matter may be appealed to the United States Circuit Court of Appeals. These procedures, too, were disregarded by the agency.

It is my firm belief that had I quietly accepted my fate and not taken an appeal from the decision of the District Office to, in effect, revoke my designation as a pilot examiner (based on three spurious reasons), the matter would have ended right there and the subsequent vendetta against me would not have been mounted. The fact that I instead sicced the US Congress and the Inspector General of the Department of Transportation on them didn't help my cause. It only served to further enrage the Office Manager at the local FSDO. However, I opted to fight by filing an appeal with the Regional Office. For this, to work with my local attorney, I retained the services of the country's leading and most knowledgeable aviation lawyer with respect to regulatory matters, John S. Yodice, who is also a personal friend.

We provided written answers to the three phony charges that the District Office had used as an excuse for taking away my designation, and, under the Freedom of Information Act, we made a demand for my file, which is maintained at the District Office. This file was fifteen inches thick when I had last seen it a few months earlier, containing hundreds of letters of commendation, many from the FAA itself, both Flight Standards and Air Traffic Control. What we received in response to our demand for the file was one-half inch thick and contained nothing but a few derogatory entries. (We have copies of over one hundred favorable entries that had been removed from this file.)

After a delay of over three months, we received a letter from the Regional Office informing us that they were changing the procedure. In an obvious effort to cover up the mistakes of the District Office by failing to provide me with adequate notice and otherwise failing to follow their own published procedures, the Regional Office stated that we would start all over again by initiating the denial of my designation at the regional level.

An appeal, the letter said, may be taken to the National Flight Standards Office in Washington, and thence to the U.S. Circuit Court of Appeals. This, of course, delayed the entire matter for an additional six months, and it took the bad guys at the District Office out of the picture. This letter dropped two of the charges that the District Office had used as an excuse to revoke my designation, and added two new ones! One of these added charges dealt with a four-and-one-half year old matter that the District Office Manager way back then had assured me, in his words, "You may consider the matter closed. You'll hear no more about it."

We were finally granted a hearing (meeting) before the Regional Flight Standards Manager. This is the same individual who was accused of ordering the destruction of records that might prove embarrassing to the FAA in another matter. John Yodice, Gary Gondek (my local counsel) and I traveled to the Regional Office to present our case.

Yodice started by asking what happened to all the favorable material that had been in my file but was no longer there. David Hanley, the Regional Flight Standards Manager, told us that files are regularly culled of stale material. John Yodice then asked, "If that's the case, how is it that five-year-old derogatory material is still there and three-week-old favorable stuff is missing?" No attempt was made to answer this question. It was simply ignored. Remember, Hanley is the same individual accused on the front page of the *New York Times* of ordering the destruction of files derogatory to the FAA.

The balance of this hearing was taken up with our satisfactorily answering each of the charges that had been used as an excuse to revoke my designation, both those of the District Office and the new ones added by the Regional Office. At the conclusion of this October meeting at the Regional Office, the Regional Flight Standards Manager, Hanley, said, "I'm tied up the rest of this week and most of next week, but I'll have an answer for you within a week or ten days."

The following month two things happened. First, I and three of the seven pilots who were flying on a contract that I had with a multinational corporation for the delivery by air of parts for its equipment received Letters of Investigation stating that there was a possible violation of FAR Part 135. Second, Inspector Sunday of my local FSDO told another aviation writer that he ought to try to take over my monthly column in **FLYING** magazine that deals with flight testing, stating that I was no longer a Pilot Examiner, having been stripped of my designation for violating Part 135! Of course, this revocation of my designation had happened almost a year before the investigation of a possible Part 135 violation had even gotten underway. Sunday further stated to that writer that the editors of **FLYING** were no doubt unaware of the fact that I was no longer an examiner and the magazine would be embarrassed to have its readers discover this. Evidently since Sunday and his boss, Hobgood, are totally devoid of honor they believe everyone else is too. When the whole business with my designation first started back in May, I had immediately notified J. Mac McClellan, the Editor-in-Chief of **FLYING** of that fact and his response was, "I don't care if you're an examiner or a former examiner, just keep writing the column!"

This column has been a sore point with some of the people at the local FSDO since I first started writing it.

It is my belief that the reason the investigation of a possible Part 135 violation was started by the FAA was to attack my pilot certificate, for without a pilot certificate I certainly couldn't be an examiner and thus my appeal of the revocation of my designation must fail. They were unaware of the fact that I had not flown a single trip on the contract, and thus no action against my pilot certificate could be taken. A few weeks after we received the Letters of Investigation, the three pilots who had been flying on the contract received letters stating that at the conclusion of the investigation no violation had been found and the matter was closed. I, however, got a letter stating that the investigation had resulted in a finding that I was guilty of being the operator of an illegal 135 operation and a Civil Penalty of Two Hundred Ninety-One Thousand dollars was assessed against me!

Please be advised that prior to entering into the contract under which I leased an airplane to the multinational corporation for its exclusive use and control, I had described in detail just how I intended to do this to two FAA General Aviation Operations Inspectors, Alfred M. Hunt and David Sunday himself. Both assured me that, as described, it did not fall under Part 135. I expected that Hunt would testify truthfully to this fact and that Sunday would, under oath, deny that I ever discussed it with him.

After the lease program had been in operation for a year and one-half, a third inspector also told me that it was not a 135 operation. At that time, early fall of 1993, the FAA took the unheard-of step of sending an Airworthiness (maintenance) Inspector not only out of his District, but out of his Region, with specific instructions to ground the airplane I had leased to the large corporation.

Meanwhile, after waiting for over five months for the answer that had been promised "within a week to ten days", we filed a Mandamus action in the federal court system requesting that the court order the FAA Regional Manager to do his duty and give us the answer he had promised "within a week to ten days."

We immediately received the expected turndown of our appeal seeking the reinstatement of my designation. This placed us in the position of being able to proceed with an appeal to the National Flight Standards Office in Washington. Even though we were promised the right to present oral argument at that level, we got our turndown on the written pleadings without benefit of oral argument. This, finally, permitted us to appeal to the Federal Circuit Court of Appeals.

We filed that appeal in the First Circuit (in Washington), and John Yodice argued the matter before the court. The FAA had maintained all along that I was entitled to Due Process. However, in their argument to the court, the FAA attorney claimed first that the court had no jurisdiction to hear the matter, and second, that if the court should take jurisdiction, I was not entitled to Due Process.

The court took jurisdiction, but agreed that I was not entitled to Due Process, in essence saying that the United States Constitution doesn't apply to the FAA. This ended my effort to regain my designation, but the matter of the Civil Penalty ($291,000 fine) was left standing. This battle was fought on the local level in the US District Court for the Southeastern District of Michigan, with Gary Gondek representing me.

For an operation to fall under Part 135 of the regulations, there must be a "holding out", and "operational control". I did not hold myself out as available for the transportation of cargo by air; rather, the multinational corporation came to me and asked if I could provide them with an airplane. I had no operational control whatever. I never knew where or when a trip was flown until after the fact when I was given the data for billing purposes.

In this battle the FAA again demonstrated the same sort of vendetta that has prevailed throughout. In all other cases of which I am aware, an airman against whom a civil penalty is imposed is permitted to compromise the penalty without an admission of guilt.

In my case, the FAA told the United States Attorney who was attempting to collect the penalty that she may compromise it out for an inconsequential amount, but only if I was willing to admit that I was guilty of the violation. This I refused to do. The US Attorney filed a motion for summary judgment, claiming that there was no issue of material fact on which to base a defense. Had this motion been granted, I would have lost and that would have ended it with me – still owing the United States $291,000. However, the judge denied the motion, which further demonstrated the weakness of the government's case.

After much negotiation with the US Attorney (who was being guided throughout by an attorney from the regional office of the FAA), the government finally offered to let me settle the matter for $10,000 if I was willing to admit to being guilty of a single count, and $20,000 without the admission of guilt! I countered by saying I would give them the $10,000 but the settlement must include the fact that there was to be no finding of guilt whatsoever. Otherwise, I was willing to take my chances at trial. The FAA, knowing they had a weak case, accepted this counter offer and the matter is finally over with.

I am now free to speak out, and I fully intend to do so. Even here the government continued to play games. The terms of the settlement were read into the record in open court, but when it came time to sign the agreement additional language was added. I had intended to sue the agency and three named inspectors (Hobgood, Sunday, and Scarpuzza), and there was no prohibition against my doing so in the agreement we reached with the United States Attorney, but language to that effect was added to the written agreement. I am not, however, prohibited from suing the individual inspectors for money damages arising from unrelated matters and I fully intend to do so. These evil people acted outside the scope of their employment with the FAA.

Having already spent over $40,000 out of pocket, not to mention the untold loss of revenue resulting from the loss of my designation as a pilot examiner and revenue from the contract with the multinational corporation which had been advised by the FAA to terminate the contract because of my alleged illegal operation, I had no funds to proceed further. Therefore, I gave them the $10,000 tribute and called an end to the fight. Of course I still intend to pursue a suit for money damages against the three named inspectors.

Here are just a couple of examples of the abuse of power as practiced by the good folks at the Detroit FSDO:

If a pilot examiner permits his designation to lapse by failing to timely renew, he or she must start all over with the initial course at OKC at his own expense. The FSDO wanted a former examiner (who had failed to renew several months previously) to be reinstated, and in order to avoid the rule that requires a former examiner to attend the initial course, they retro-dated his application to indicate timely renewal. An examiner is designated for private, commercial, and instrument-airplane authority, but for each specific make and model of twin he/she must have a letter of authority. An examiner with no Cessna 310 authority solicited a 310 student for his flight test, and when asked if she had 310 authority replied, "No, but all I have to do is call Inspector Dave Sunday, and he'll authorize it." This is, of course, contrary to the method by which such authority is obtained.

The old saying that power corrupts and absolute power corrupts absolutely has never been truer than in the case of the Flight Standards Division of the FAA. Individuals in the agency continue to abuse the unbridled power that I'm certain the Congress never intended them to have. I have been consistently lied to by employees of the FAA -- from inspectors at the local district level to the head of Flight Standards at the region, to the top guy in Flight Standards at the national level. I had thought that at least above the district level I would encounter people of integrity, but it didn't take very long for me to become disillusioned. I learned that at all levels there are people totally devoid of honor.

It is indeed a sad state of affairs when an agency of the government is so intimidating that it has its own employees terrorized. As an example, several inspectors, throughout my ordeal, privately confided that they knew the entire matter was a setup but were afraid to come forward for fear of what it would do to their careers. Along the same line, several lawyers who specialize in aviation matters and who are also pilots, backed off from representing me for fear of reprisals against their own pilot certificates.

Somehow this unbridled power that the FAA has taken unto

itself must be curbed; these people must be made accountable for their actions. As the former Inspector General for the Department of Transportation, Mary Schiavo, put it, "The FAA has created a culture of nonaccountability!"

> ***"I'm not interested in safety. That's the job
> of the National Transportation Safety Board.
> My job is to find violations,
> and that's just what I intend to do!"***
> **Aviation Safety Inspector George DeMartini**

# Busted !

Although my treatment at the hands of the agency has been nothing less than disgraceful, what was done to me was discretionary. Of course my contention has been that the agency abused its discretion, but the court held that the Administrator's discretion is absolute and cannot be abused.

However, a case has come to my attention that has much more far-reaching implications for the average airperson because it could happen to anyone who holds a pilot certificate.

The facts are as follows:

Kenneth B., a former naval pilot with over 1065 hours of experience, decided to acquire certification as a civilian pilot. He enrolled in a ground school course conducted by Michael J. Taylor. In 1993, on completion of this course, he took and passed the Private Pilot Written Examination with a score of 90%.

On January 28, 1995, Mr. B. began to undertake flight instruction from Taylor. Prior to starting this training, Mike Taylor sought the advice and counsel of the local FSDO (Flight Standards District Office of the FAA) with respect to just what would be required. He was told that he needed only prep the applicant for the skill requirement (Practical Test) since the experience requirement had already been met. Taylor gave Kenneth B. 5.8 hours (tach time) dual instruction before permitting him to solo, and Mr. B. had 3.5 tach hours of local solo time before Taylor prepped him for cross-country with 1.5 tach hours of dual instruction. This 1.5 tach time equates to about an hour and fifty-five minutes of actual clock time.

Please be advised that, as a Certified Flight Instructor, I have personally trained and recommended for certification numerous former military pilots, who, having met the experience requirement (regardless of how long in the past) and the knowledge requirement by having passed the appropriate written, required only sufficient training to meet the skill requirement. In some cases this amounted to merely brushing up on the maneuvers.

It should also be noted that between 1969 and 1974 Mr. B., as a naval aviator, flew in excess of 1000 hours in combat aircraft, and executed 185 carrier landings. He was a Landing Safety Officer (LSO) on the USS Forestal. From 1975 through 1981 he was a full performance level FAA Center Radar Controller, and from 1984 through 1995 he was a senior training analyst developing and teaching aviation training programs. He literally "wrote the book" on aerial navigation, and since that time he has been a professional educator.

Mike Taylor is a professional educator and part-time flight instructor, formerly with Eastern Airlines. He is the holder of an Airline Transport Pilot Certificate, Certified Flight Instructor Certificate, Flight Engineer Certificate, and Mechanic Certificate. He has sponsored several FAA Safety Programs by arranging for a site for these presentations and otherwise participating, and he has been nominated for Flight Instructor of the Year honors in his local FSDO. Are you getting a message here? It seems that the bad guys in the FAA single out for persecution the most prominent aviators (Bob Hoover, the world's premier aviator; me, the most **visible** pilot examiner in the world because of my column in *FLYING*; and Mike Taylor, one of the more prominent instructors in his district). I suppose these little people in the FAA somehow think that a demonstration of raw power by knocking down a Hoover increases their stature. What it really does is draw the scorn and contempt of the entire aviation community upon them.

In preparing Ken B. for his Private Pilot practical test, Mike gave Ken training in cross-country operations, although this was not required by the regulations, since Ken had already met all the experience requirements for the certificate (FAR 61.41). A few days after having administered this training, Mike reviewed Ken's planning and dispatched him on a solo cross-country trip, after making the appropriate endorsements and logbook entries.

Ken, who owned the airplane, was advised by Mike to top off the fuel tanks at the destination prior to starting the return trip, and he so testified.

However, because of the lateness of the hour, Ken visually checked the remaining fuel and determined that he had enough, including reserve, for the trip home, so he departed without adding fuel. You guessed it. He ran out of fuel some sixteen miles short of his home airport, resulting in an unscheduled, off-airport landing. There was no injury, but the aircraft was severely damaged. That his navigation skill is excellent is demonstrated by the fact that the off airport landing happened right on the centerline of the airway he was tracking home. This incident, of course, precipitated an investigation by the Friendly Feds in the form of an Aviation Safety Inspector by the name of George DeMartini, who is alleged to have told Mike Taylor that he was not interested in safety; rather, his job was to find violations, and that's just what he intended to do in this matter!

Actually, the first inkling Mike had that a violation was under consideration was when he received a Letter of Investigation (LOI) from DeMartini stating that a violation may have occurred and Mike may have been involved (the usual boilerplate). The LOI was sent to Mike's correct address by Certified Mail, Return Receipt Requested, under date of March 21, 1995. In a spirit of cooperation (I believe this is a mistake. Any effort to cooperate with these evil people is interpreted as a sign of weakness, leading them to push even harder.), Mike Taylor responded to the LOI with an explanation of the training he had given Ken. He both wrote and telephoned DeMartini in an effort to resolve the matter. However, DeMartini pressed on.

In his investigation, Inspector DeMartini examined Ken's pilot logbook and noted that a few days prior to the cross-country flight in question, Taylor had flown with Ken a total of 1.5 tach hours (the equivalent of 1.9 or more clock hours), and that the training on this flight included cross-country navigation, emergency procedures, and other tasks in the Private Pilot Practical Test Standards. This flight had taken place on February 3, 1995.

DeMartini also noted that on the day of the accident flight

(February 11, 1995), Taylor had reviewed Ken's cross-country planning and preparation prior to signing him off for the trip. Somehow, DeMartini seems to hold the impression that there is something wrong with signing a student off for cross-country flight without administering **flight instruction** on that same day. He makes a big issue of the fact that Ken only got ground instruction on the day of the flight. He also claims that 1.5 tach hours is insufficient time to accomplish all the procedures and maneuvers that both Taylor and Ken testified were completed on the day of the flight training. (Taylor claims that even this wasn't really "training" but rather an evaluation of the procedures and maneuvers of an accomplished pilot.)

Taylor says that DeMartini indicated on the telephone that he was not interested in safety, that's the duty of the NTSB. His job, he said, is to find violations and that's just what he is doing. The next Taylor heard of the affair was when he received a letter signed by Naomi Tsuda, Associate Regional Counsel for the FAA, stating, "You may not have received the Notice of Proposed Certificate Action *allegedly* issued by this office on August 2, 1995." This letter was dated November 9, 1995 and was received by Taylor two days later. It should be noted here that this letter proposed to "suspend your **Flight Instructor** Authorization for a period of ninety (90) days" (emphasis added).

The FAA's Regional Counsel's Office claims to have first sent a Notice of Proposed Certificate Action on August 3, 1995 by Registered Mail, Return Receipt Requested. No receipt was returned to the FAA, nor was the letter itself, if indeed such a letter was ever sent. If there was such a letter, it was certainly never received by Taylor. It would have to have been beyond six months of the time of the alleged violation, which occurred on February 3. (The letter, claimed by the FAA to have been written August 2 and mailed August 3, could not possibly have been received by Taylor until August 4th or 5th at the earliest.)

Finally waking up to the fact that DeMartini meant business and that full, complete cooperation was getting him nowhere, Mike Taylor retained the services of an attorney. The next step was an informal conference by telephone involving Taylor's attorney Garland O. Bell, Inspector DeMartini, and FAA Attorney Tsuda. Bell, also naively (and mistakenly) believing that he was dealing with reasonable people, attempted to settle the matter informally by explaining just how none of Mike's actions or omissions constituted a violation of any regulations. Mike, who was not informed of its scheduling, did not participate in this telephone conference. The FAA pressed on, and Mike's attorney requested a hearing before an NTSB Administrative Law Judge (ALJ), the next step in the process. It was at this point that the proposed certificate suspension was expanded from his Flight Instructor Certificate only to **all** of Mike's FAA certificates. Mike was charged with giving inadequate cross country training!

NTSB rule 821.33, the so-called "Stale Complaint Rule" is really a statute of limitations limiting the time frame within which the FAA may seek sanctions against an airperson to six months from the time a violation is discovered. The rule states that notice of a sanction against an airperson must be **received** by the airman within six months of the date of the occurrence from which the violation arose. There are two very specific exceptions that allow the FAA to impose sanctions sometime beyond the six month period, neither of which applies in this case. Therefore, based on NTSB Rule 821.33, Mike Taylor's attorney moved for a dismissal of the FAA's complaint against his client. This motion was opposed by the FAA and denied by the ALJ. Prior to the hearing, one of the charges was dropped as being stale, but the other was allowed to stand.

At the hearing before the ALJ, Patrick G. Geraghty, both Mike Taylor and Ken B. testified under oath that the training Mr. B. received was adequate. They also both testified that Taylor had instructed Kenny to fill up his fuel tanks prior to starting his return trip.

DeMartini testified that the training was inadequate. Taylor's attorney was prevented by the ALJ from cross-examining DeMartini regarding the means by which he had determined the training to be inadequate. Judge Geraghty opted to believe the testimony of DeMartini, who was not present when the training took place, and to disbelieve both Taylor and Ken B., who were there. He therefore ruled in favor of the FAA, but dropped the proposed suspension from ninety to sixty days, but added **all** of Taylor's FAA certificates as the FAA was now demanding, not merely his Flight Instructor Certificate, as was originally proposed.

This decision paved the way for an appeal to the full NTSB, and

Taylor appealed. Unless the evidence is completely overwhelming, the Board is very reluctant to overturn a decision of one of its ALJs, and although in this case the evidence does indeed seem to be overwhelming, the Board opted to uphold Geraghty's decision, and it was affirmed by the full Board. The next step is to appeal the Board's decision to the United States Circuit Court of Appeals, and the matter now stands before the Ninth Circuit where a hearing is to be held in the reasonably near future.

The problem now is that the court, of course, won't hear evidence, but may only consider the question of whether or not the Board erred in affirming the decision of the ALJ. In fact, the only issue before the court is that of the stale complaint rule. The facts that training was not required, and that even so the training was adequate and complete, can't be considered. Here again, the court is very reluctant to overturn the decision of a lower court (in this case the NTSB) without clear and compelling reasons, and there is some law allowing the FAA to circumvent the stale complaint rule where the failure of the Postal Service to deliver the notice was the cause of the delay. We will just have to wait and see what the court does.

In this account of Mike Taylor's battle with the agency, I have omitted numerous motions at all levels entered by both the FAA and Taylor, but these motions have all been procedural in nature rather than substantive. To detail them would have added nothing to the story.

The thing to remember is that way back when the Congress of the United States created the CAA (Civil Aeronautics Authority), predecessor of the FAA, the agency was charged with the responsibility (read "duty") to "foster and encourage the development and growth of civil aviation in the United States." Way down the list the agency was authorized (read "allowed") to promulgate and enforce regulations pertaining to safety in air commerce. Over the years since that founding of the agency, it has moved farther and farther away from fostering and encouraging development and growth. Now, almost the entire energy of the agency is devoted to promulgating and enforcing regulations -- many of which have nothing whatever to do with safety. The claim is often made that an airperson has endangered the life or property of another when there is nobody anywhere around to endanger. As in the Taylor case, the FAA, in order to make a violation stick, changes its interpretation of the regulations to fit the facts, just as DeMartini did here. If the rules don't permit them to do what they want, they just change the rules (or how the rules are interpreted).

As a direct result of this activity on the part of the FAA, an adversarial position has arisen between the aviation community and the agency. Because of the high-handed, devious manner in which the agency traps pilots and operators into admitting wrongdoing, we have reached a point at which virtually nobody in the entire aviation community trusts the FAA. That's too bad; it should be a partnership between the providers and the users.

### The Davy Crocker Story

The treatment of one airman at the hands of the folks in Flight Standards (the Friendly Feds) goes far beyond shocking, and beyond disgusting. It is downright sickening! Grover Cleveland Crocker (known to his friends as "Davy") had served his country well for many years, first in the military, and then as a FAA inspector. Yes, he had been one of their own, but that didn't stop them from trampling all over him to get at someone else they wanted to persecute.

After a long and distinguished career of service to his government Davy Crocker retired, first from the military, and then from the FAA. Sure he's a double dipper, but so what? He earned every dime of the retirement pay he's drawing, and he's entitled to supplement it with earnings from his activity as a Designated Pilot Examiner. But the government he has served so faithfully has turned on him, or at least one representative of that government and the agency for which that representative works. And because the bureaucracy protects its own, the agency has closed ranks behind this vicious individual who went through Crocker to get at his real targets.

Inspector Smith in Alaska, like Inspector DeMartini in Arizona, and Inspector Sunday in Detroit, seems to make up his own rules as he goes along. DeMartini in Arizona arbitrarily (and all on his own despite overwhelming evidence to the contrary) decided that the cross-country training given by Mike Taylor was insufficient (even though no cross-country training at all was required). Sunday in Detroit decided that my lease agreement with the multinational firm was a Part 135 operation. Likewise, Smith in Alaska arbitrarily and, again despite overwhelming evidence to the contrary, decided that Davy Crocker, back in Texas, had given inadequate flight tests to two airmen.

Because Crocker had been a military check pilot, qualified in a large variety of aircraft, he was a very desirable asset to the FAA, which he served faithfully for a number of years. On his retirement from the FAA, he became a DPE (Designated Pilot Examiner), and he was authorized to issue certificates and ratings in a substantial number of somewhat exotic airplanes. It should be noted that at one point he was criticized for being too lenient as an examiner, but his answer to that was that the quality of applicants who came to him for type ratings was very high and most of them were very well qualified for the ratings they sought. On the whole, the applicants he served were well qualified professional pilots seeking ATP certification and type ratings, so the vast majority of them might be expected to pass their checkrides.

Although Crocker's designation as an examiner was through the San Antonio District Office of the FAA, with the proper clearance[1] he examined two applicants at Love Field Dallas, Texas on August 30, 1996. These two applicants were from Alaska and were seeking to have type ratings in the IA Jet aircraft (N240AA, an Aero Commander Model 1121 – Jet Commander) added to their Airline Transport Pilot Certificates. This aircraft is rare enough that there are very few examiners qualified to administer type rating tests in it. The two applicants worked for a charter operator in Alaska, Alaska Island Air (AIA), which had as its Principal Operations Inspector from the FAA (POI) a certain David A. Smith, who worked out of the Fairbanks Alaska Flight Standards District Office (FSDO). The two applicants had come to the lower forty-eight to pick up the airplane, have it added to their company's charter certificate, and get type rated to fly it.

Unknown to Crocker, Inspector Smith from the Fairbanks, Alaska, FSDO was at that time investigating the activities of the company for which the two pilots worked, as well as several of its

---

[1] A pilot examiner is designated to administer flight tests within the geographic confines of his own district office, but with advance clearance from both his district and the district in which the test is to be conducted, he may give flight tests in another district. In Crocker's case, his Designated Pilot Examiner card was signed off for giving flight tests in the Dallas area as well as the San Antonio area-a somewhat unique but not unheard-of procedure.

pilots, including Michael A. Spisak and Alan G. Larson, the two pilots examined by Crocker. Smith's obvious intent was to shut down the operations of AIA. Both pilots passed their checkrides.

When Spisak and Larson returned to Alaska with the airplane and their new ratings, Inspector David A. Smith of the Fairbanks Flight Standards District Office of the FAA requested that the Dallas FSDO forward to him the paperwork surrounding their checkrides for the type ratings. Upon receipt and examination of the FAA Form 8710.1s (Application for Certificate or Rating), Inspector Smith yanked the certificates of both pilots and demanded that the San Antonio FSDO revoke Davy Crocker's designation as a pilot examiner, claiming fraud and misrepresentation on Crocker's part. The San Antonio FSDO suspended Crocker's designation pending their investigation. In November 1996, at the conclusion of the local investigation in Texas, the San Antonio Flight Standards District Office restored the designation, stating that Crocker had satisfactorily answered all the questions posed by Inspector Smith.

This should have been the end of Crocker's troubles, but the viciousness of Inspector Smith decreed otherwise. Here's how the entire sordid story unfolds:

On August 10, 1996 the two airmen, Spisak and Larson, came to Davy Crocket to have type ratings for the IA-JET (Jet Commander) added to their ATP Certificates. Following the examiners manual and the Practical Test Standards (PTS) for such checkrides, Crocker administered practical tests to both applicants. He gave them a joint oral (a recommended procedure), and had them both occupy the two pilot seats in the airplane (also a recommended procedure) while he observed their performance. The flight originated and terminated at Dallas Love Field (DAL), Texas. The air work was performed *en route* to Greenville, TX, Majors Field (GVT), and the applicants changed seats in the air midway on the trip so that Crocker could observe the performance of both pilots as they did the air work. They changed seats again after the first pilot had completed his approaches. Each pilot executed seven instrument approaches at GVT, and the eighth and final approach was accomplished by each pilot back at DAL.

The weather was clear with light winds and the layout of the airport at GVT is such that they could land on runway 17, rollout to the end, turn around and take off RWY 35 and fly directly to the approach fix. GVT has ILS, NDB, and VOR approaches to RWY 17. The VOR intersects RWY 17 at a 50 degree angle, which provides an excellent opportunity for a circling approach. Several TASKS of the PTS were combined (another recommended procedure), including a VOR engine out, no flap, circle to land approach, Since GVT has Runway Markers, it is possible for a pilot to execute an aborted take-off and know that he still has balanced field length to stop and then continue the take-off.

The entire flight test for the two pilots consumed 2.7 hours block time. (My own multiengine ATP checkride, conducted by a very strict FAA Inspector, lasted 1.2 hours and included all the approaches with everything working and all the approaches with one engine caged, including a single engine landing to a full stop from an ILS approach). Both of Crocket's applicants were well-qualified instrument pilots. They were current Part 135 pilots in the King Air and the Caravan. Both held ATP Certificates with type ratings for the DC-3, and had flown the DC-3 in Air Carrier Operations in Kotzebue, Alaska, and in Davy's own words, "If you don't know where that is, go NW of Nome, AL and find it. From Kotzebue, walk west a short distance and your hat floats. Continue west, if you are any kind of a swimmer, and you'll find yourself in Russia. I was testing two very proficient instrument pilots." He logged 1.6 and 1.8 hours respectively on the two applications (8710.1). Please be advised that Inspector Smith himself had, just fourteen days earlier, traveled from Fairbanks to Kotzebue and administered a complete Part 135 flight check (almost the same as a type rating checkride) to Mike Spisak in a King Air. They were in the air a total of 56 minutes, block time came to 73 minutes. Smith logged 1.4 hours for this flight and at Crocker's hearing testified that he had merely rounded up. (Note: Crocker says the guidelines require that you round to the nearest tenth, but I was told to always round *down* to the next lower tenth. Crocker also points out that Smith could use some remedial math).

When the two pilots got back to Alaska they began operating the airplane as an air ambulance vehicle. It had been configured for this work with a stretcher and patient oxygen, and was in the process of being changed from the AAN certificate to the IAI Certificate, a process that normally takes one day. Smith told the operator that it would take him five or six weeks to complete the paperwork for the changeover. Prior to the change being completed, an emergency call was received and they transported a seriously ill native boy to Fairbanks in the airplane, still operating on the AAN Certificate, but the company had had its name and logo painted on the aircraft. This is a no-no, and a competitor at Kotzebue reported this to the Fairbanks FSDO (Inspector Smith). Smith saw his chance and leaped at the opportunity to nail the operator and the two pilots. However, in order to get at the pilots, he would have to go through Crocker and demonstrate that the pilots were improperly certified to fly the Jet Commander by virtue of having had inadequate checkrides administered by Crocker.

As a bit of further insight into Smith's character and ignorance regarding his job, when he saw Davy's name on the two temporary certificates, he set out to locate Crocker. In Davy's own words, here is how he went about it "In one affidavit, David Smith was trying to show me as a very slippery examiner. He states that when he saw Spisak and Larson had temporary certificates with my name on them, he started to try and find me to see if I was really an examiner. He says he contacted the Dallas Office, since I had given the checks in that district. And DAL FSDO said they had no knowledge of me, try HOU. (I had retired from the DAL FSDO and now they didn't know me!) He then states that HOU told him to try SAT FSDO. And, lo and behold, he found me. I wonder what he thinks that little block, down in the right hand corner (of the temporary certificate) with SW-17008 (an examiner designation number, readily available to anyone seeking information) indicates. Could he be that ignorant, or merely trying to make the reader think I was a bad actor?"

David Smith therefore embarked on a most vicious, vindictive investigation of the type rating flights, ignoring every items of evidence that the PTS had been complied with in all respects. During the investigation he suppressed or withheld several items of evidence (Sound familiar? Remember my own case and that of Mike Taylor?)

At Smith's insistence, Davy Crocker's authority to conduct flight tests was suspended. He was then interviewed by Holly Geiger, San Antonio Flight Standards District Office Operations Unit Manager and Sam Munn, the Principal Operations Inspector assigned to supervise his activity. He submitted to this interview without counsel because he had conducted the flight tests in question in full compliance with the PTS. A few days later Sam Munn called and advised him that he could go back to administering flight tests. This was followed in writing by a letter from Holly Geiger confirming that his examining authority was restored.

According to Munn, when David Smith learned that Davy had been cleared of all charges, he "went ballistic." He demanded that Crocker's designation as an examiner again be suspended, claiming to have additional evidence (not a true statement). Consequently, Holly Geiger sent Davy another letter ordering him to cease all testing, pending the outcome of further investigation. Smith used the fact that Crocker had given the two airmen joint oral quizzing during the conduct of the exams, as his excuse to deny the two type ratings, and Geiger concurred in this. (Note: As an examiner I have often conducted joint orals for two applicants. It *is* an approved procedure.) Again, in Crocker's own words:

*The egregious lack of knowledge by both David A. Smith and Holly Geiger was that a group oral could be conducted for a two pilot aircraft. When Holly interviewed me, she handed me a list of questions from David A. Smith. When did each oral start and when did it end? When I answered that I had conducted them together, Holly frowned but said nothing. When she concluded the interview, I asked her if she had a problem with the group oral and she replied that she wasn't sure about it. (She sure didn't object to it when I typed her and another inspector in 1985 in the IA-Jet Simulator at Simuflite.) I handed her the printout of the Inspector's Handbook which not only authorizes it, but says it is the preferred method for crew coordination.*

Smith used the fact of them having been given a joint oral as the basis for the revocation of the two airmen's certification as well as his attack on Crocker. He filed eleven violation cases in all, ten against AIA and its pilots and one against Davy Crocker. Davy attempted to have his matter investigated locally (in Texas) but, contrary to normal procedure, Smith had had it transferred to himself. (Crocker was told, "When the Division Managers get together, they can pretty much do what they want. The handbook sorta goes out the window.") (Does this sound familiar? Remember, in my own fight to retain my designation as a Pilot Examiner they kept changing the procedure in midstream, each change being contrary to the printed procedures in the manual.)

Sometime in December of 1996, Smith figured out that the joint oral is an approved procedure, so he shifted his attack on Crocker to the amount of time spent on the flight checks. He attempted to prove, with perjured testimony, that Crocker could not have been in Dallas long enough to administer the two checkrides. The actual charge against Davy was that he had made false and fraudulent entries on the Airman Applications (8710.1). In April of 1997 Alaska filed an Emergency Revocation Order on Crocker's Pilot Certificates (this was eleven months after the flight tests. Where's the emergency, the imminent danger to the public?) At this time Crocker was told by Holly Geiger that as soon as he was cleared of all charges, his designation as an examiner would be restored, another lie.

At the hearing, Administrative Law Judge Mullins ruled that the FAA's case had no merit, and he found in favor of Crocker. (By the bye, David A. Smith lost all ten of the other cases he had brought against AIA and its pilots.) The FAA appealed Judge Mullin's Order and Opinion in the Crocker case, and the full National Transportation Safety Board unanimously upheld the ALJ, also stating that the FAA case against Davy Crocker was without merit, Davy then filed a claim for reimbursement under the Equal Access to Justice Act (EAJA) and was awarded thirty-seven thousand eight hundred thirty-seven dollars and forty-seven cents ($37,837.47) for attorney fees and expenses in defending himself against this spurious action. The FAA has appealed this award at the time of this writing. Over a year has passed and that appeal is still pending.

Meanwhile, back at the San Antonio FSDO, Davy asked that his designation be restored as promised. However, in an apparent attempt to placate Smith, this was denied. The excuse offered for this denial was that, in the face of overwhelming evidence to the contrary, an examiner in Crocker's area is not needed. As this is being written, Davy Crocker is still fighting the good fight, attempting to get his designation as a pilot examiner restored. I certainly hope he is more successful than I was!

### Finally, A (Short) Horror Story

As an example of how they go after those airmen with prominent names, here is what happened to Richard Jeppesen (Name sound familiar? Yep, he's the son of the one and only original guy who drew the first approaches for air carrier pilots): I will let him tell the story in his own words.

*"I have been in a four year battle with the Orlando FSDO, only to find out that the FAA can lie, fabricate, change pleadings, etc., and there is no apparent forum that is available to aviators to expose these Gestapo tactics. There is no accountability, there is no place a citizen can be heard or due process gained against the FAA or an FAA Inspector. Therefore, it is my opinion that rouge and dishonest inspectors answer to no one. Although the FAA has many excellent, well-trained people, the pot is stained by the bad elements that exist within the agency. I have talked with many inspectors who are friends of mine. They know who the bad apples are, but nothing can be done to remove them from service, and all inspectors know this. They are aware that nothing can be done to them, so if they encounter a personality conflict that perhaps grows into a vendetta, or maybe the inspector is simply full of himself and the power he wields, the inspector can do as he pleases. If the citizen, the aviator, attempts to expose these people, he has nowhere to turn. Worse, he finds himself under attack, harassed, investigated, and threatened.*

*I own a forty passenger F-27 that we use to fly medical doctors to give free eye exams and free glasses to kids who can't see clearly enough to read. When I bought the aircraft, the facility that had worked on it since 1984 accomplished the annual inspection and signed it off. I found later that this inspection had been severely 'pencil whipped', including not replacing time-limited parts, and signing off inspections of parts that were not even on the airplane. I sued them, and three years later they settled in court for $185,000 and I can tell you they wouldn't have paid this amount if we didn't have the evidence against them. Now we had the depositions, the evidence, etc.*

*When I went to the FAA and told them what this repair station had done, the only question was, 'Did you fly the airplane?' They wanted to violate me! Can you believe that? I am the one who found all this stuff wrong. I am the one who fixed it. I am the one who exposed the repair facility. I am the one that spent three years of my life in litigation, and the FAA wants to violate me! Frankly, if the FAA inspector who was in charge of oversight of this huge facility had done his job, even partially, I would not have had to do any of this. How did the airplane sneak out of this facility right under the nose of the FAA? Quite a message the FAA sends. 'Don't tell us about a facility that we have a dedicated inspector overseeing. It makes us look bad.'*

*This repair facility does contract maintenance on airliners all the time. They are big, and they are turning out aircraft that I believe, based on my experience, can't begin to be airworthy. My log books looked excellent, but nobody is checking the work. The FAA, it appears, in this facility, only looks at the paperwork. They don't check anything.*

*After the Orlando FSDO threatened me, I took the story to Washington and they forced Orlando to grant me immunity so that I could show them what we had found. This made Orlando, specifically a Keith May (head of legal), very upset. So the stage was set. The FAA was about to attack.*

*I filed five complaint letters with the FAA about the FAA tactics and never received a response. When a complaint is filed with Washington, it is sent back to the FSDO about which the complaint has been filed, and if they throw it in the wastebasket that's the end of the story. Quite a system, huh? When I tried to discuss this with the manager of the FSDO, his response was, 'You're wasting your time.' I therefore turned my evidence over to the Inspector General's office. They are (slowly) working on the case. This action also made the Orlando FSDO mad.*

*So the message to the aviation community is very clear: Never, never complain about the FAA or they will attack you. And attack they have, Within thirty days of discovering that I had gone to the IG with my complaint, they sent four inspectors out to try to ground the airplane. (Sound familiar? That's just what they did to me when I had the temerity to stand up to them.)*

*They couldn't find anything wrong, so two inspectors came out to inspect the logbooks. One of them, Tom Littleton by name, was as far removed from being a gentleman as I have seen to date. There was an independent witness to his accusatory attitude, and the man actually became belligerent with my wife. Again, they could find nothing wrong. In order to ground the airplane Littleton, supported by his boss, Bob Cunningham revoked our letter of deviation, grounding the airplane because the inspection program was faulty. This is the same inspection program that had been approved and in place for sixteen years, and twice approved by the Orlando FSDO. When asked what they wanted changed, a letter-writing contest begins asked in writing what they wanted changed and never got a response. Littleton just wouldn't tell me.*

*Littleton just ordered us to rewrite the program and submit it for approval. So I did. Twice. And got turned down both times. All this ate up several months.*

*Finally, I went to Washington (since Atlanta, the Regional Office, appears to rubber stamp everything Orlando does) and I found the other FAA in the person of Richard Gordon, Deputy Director of Flight Standards--an honorable gentleman who does not subscribe to these tactics. He asked an inspector from the Miami FSDO, Bob Schrard, to investigate the situation. We spent a day together while he looked at the airplane and the records. He then spent a day with the enemy. Some three months later, the approval came through. No changes whatever were required, and the letter of deviation was reissued. How can that be? Our program was either bad or it wasn't. I got my airplane back into the air, but it required Washington to overrule Orlando to do it."*

## Conclusion

Several basic principles can be distilled from these "horror stories" of the treatment of airmen at the hands of the Flight Standards Division of the FAA.

**First:** When one evil inspector with an agenda of his own goes after an airman, the agency closes ranks and backs him up, no matter what lies are required or what regulations have to be bent or ignored.

**Second:** It is the prominent and well-known airmen who are most likely to be victimized by an evil inspector.

**Third:** Former or retired inspectors are also particularly susceptible to attack.

**Fourth:** To paraphrase Shakespeare, they can lie and smile whiles they lie and cry "content" to that which grieves their hearts (if they have hearts and consciences at all.)

**Fifth:** Most inspectors (not just the *really* bad guys) won't hesitate to make up rules to fit their own agendas without regard to whether or not such regulations exist.

**Sixth:** Administrative Law Judges are prone to place much more credence on the testimony of FAA Inspectors than anyone else (after all, he's an FAA Inspector and he ought to know what he's talking about.)

**Seventh:** The NTSB is very reluctant to reverse the decisions of the ALJs, even in the face of overwhelming evidence to the contrary.

**Eighth:** The United States Circuit Courts of Appeals are most reluctant to overturn (reverse) the NTSB.

> ***Once an inspector gets after an airman, he or she, guilty or not, has a decidedly uphill battle!***

What certificate holders must understand is an airman certificate is a privilege and not a right. Thus, they are not entitled to the protection of the constitution (due process, etc.) I don't say this is as it should be; it certainly isn't, but that's the way it is. If an airman certificate were in fact a license, it would be different.

PART 3
SUCCESS!

## Chapter 3

## A Success Story

Pilot Wins, FAA Loses

" I Surrender ! "

After relating a couple of horror stories about cases in which the FAA prosecuted certificate actions against apparently-innocent airmen, I am, for a refreshing change, able to relate a man-bites-dog tale in which an airman took on the FAA and actually won! The full verbatim transcript of Darryl Phillips' trial before NTSB Judge Mullins, plus some "rest of the story" comments by Phillips are also presented. Mr. Phillips graciously permitted me to use this material with the stipulation that I tell the story in its entirety and in his own words.

First, however, I should tell you what I know about a couple of the NTSB ALJs with whom I am familiar. One of them is a nice old man who knows absolutely nothing about aviation, and has been known to sleep quietly through the testimony being offered at his hearings. Because of his lack of knowledge, this man is inclined to almost automatically rule in favor of the FAA. The other, whom I know personally and consider a good friend, is Judge W. Roger Mullins. Mullins is a certificated pilot, and is knowledgeable in matters aeronautical. He applies logic and reason to his decisions and quite frequently rules against the FAA and in favor of the airman. (He also gets reversed on occasion by the full Board.)

### Pilot Wins, FAA Loses

As Mike Busch, Editor-in-Chief of **Avweb,** the on-line weekly aviation news bulletin, put it, *"It's refreshing to read this man-bites-dog tale in which an airman took on the FAA and actually won! In this case, the airman was well-known aviation iconoclast Darryl Phillips, and his career wasn't exactly at stake but an important issue was: whether FAA orders and regulations take precedence over public law as formulated by Congress, or vice-versa. The story of how Darryl single-handedly prevailed over the FAA's bureaucratic absurdity (without a lawyer, by the way) makes fascinating reading... and just might offer some valuable lessons about dealing with the Feds."*

The following is Darryl's story in his own words:

Basically, the facts are these: After 30+ years of power flying, I qualified for an aero-tow glider rating last Christmas. The training package was my Christmas gift from my wife Patsy. We spent the holiday with good friends Phil and Marge Hodge, who had just completed their own landing strip in eastern Tennessee. All four of us are pilots, plus Marge has a couple of Pat's horses, so we have a lot in common. On top of that, Phil and I got our glider training. It was a great trip.

### Is Rural Living Against FAA Regs?

After passing the checkride at Chilhowee Gliderport on December 27 1996, I filled out certificate application form 8710-1, which specifically states "FAA policy requires that you use your permanent mailing address". My address is:

Darryl H. Phillips
Rt. 2, Box 255
Sallisaw, OK 74955-9654

I've lived there for years, have no plans to move, and that is the address I used. Per the usual practice, I surrendered my pilot certificate and received a temporary, good for 120 days.

In February, the FAA Airmen Certification Branch in OKC bounced the application. They wanted a map of how to find my residence. They cited Action Notice 8700.2, which states that FAA must get a map from anyone who has a rural address.

I did some checking and couldn't find any requirement in the regulations for a map. So I refused... and the battle was on.

My 120-day temporary certificate expired, and for a while I couldn't fly at all, even though there was no allegation that I had committed any infraction or violation.

I filed an appeal -- they call it a "petition" in the case of certificate denial -- with NTSB (docket CD-33), and Friday, September 5, a hearing was held before Administrative Law Judge Mullins in Oklahoma City.

## The FAA Wimps Out

FAA attorney Joseph Standell made the perfunctory motion for summary judgment. I argued to the contrary. We each made our opening statements. Since I was the appealing party, I went first. I had subpoenaed quite a bit of material from FAA, and had my ducks in a row.

Fortunately, there is a burden on the appellant (me) to show that FAA actions are "arbitrary, capricious, or otherwise not in accord with law". This is great, because it opens the door to demonstrating all sorts of FAA actions that fall in that category. I was prepared to show that the Orders (such as 8700.1, 871 SAC, 86] 0.4F, 8400.1, and others) are illegal. Plus a lot more.

I began to enter items into evidence. I hadn't even called my first witness (the two witnesses I had subpoenaed were both FAA employees at Airmen Certification Branch), when the FAA attorney suddenly announced that I could have my certificate. Bam! It was all over. All the work I had gone through to prepare myself for the hearing, all the evidence I had amassed, all the adrenaline I had flowing... it didn't matter, it was all over. I had won.

The very interesting thing was watching the FAA attorney. His most important objective was to see that my evidence did not make it into the record. The FAA is far more interested in covering up their mistakes than they are in justice. To say nothing of aviation safety.

### What The Judge Never Heard

Briefly, here is some of what I was going to demonstrate to the court:

1. In 1988, Congress passed Public Law 100-690. A portion of that law is entitled the "Federal Aviation Administration Drug Enforcement Assistance Act". It requires FAA to particularly watch pilot certificate applications that use a "post office box" or "mail drop".

2. In response to the above, FAA's Robert L. Goodrich issued Action Notice 8700.2 in August 1989. Apparently, Mr. Goodrich didn't have a clue as to what a "mail drop" was, so he wrote the order to cover post office boxes and rural routes! A mail drop is usually a business (such as Mail Boxes Etc.) where a recipient can receive mail without revealing his whereabouts. However, Goodrich made no mention of mail drops at all in 8700.2. And as we have seen so often in the FAA, once they make a mistake -- even an innocent mistake -- they cannot and will not reverse course and correct the error. It turns out that Goodrich's 8700.2 expired August 18, 1990, but is still cited today by the FAA as justification to deny a certificate.

3. Since 1988, FAA has done absolutely nothing to obey the law regarding mail drops. In a superficial Internet search, I easily found 23 pilots who use mail drops in the Miami, Florida area, a known drug hub.

I also found 74 (no kidding, 74) certificates of pilots who claim to reside in the same suite in Miami. Curious? Hop over to the AVweb database section and search pilot certificates at zip code 33134. You will be amazed, maybe amazed enough to send a copy of that list of Ricci Riccardos to your congressman. Or the DEA.

Of course, living in Miami does not make you a drug smuggler. Having a Hispanic name doesn't make you a drug smuggler. Even being a pilot doesn't make you a drug smuggler (we've been trying to convey that message for a long time). But this list should indicate that FAA Airman Certification Branch is not paying much attention to the law.

4. Since the law was passed, FAA policy diverged. On one hand, the regulations are in accord with the law. Until the recent Part 61 rewrite, there was only one regulation that applied to this, 61.13(a). Now there are two more, 61.29(d)(2) and 61.35(a)(2)(iv). In each case, they support the intent of Congress in PL 100-690 in fighting the war on drugs. On the other hand, there are many FAA orders such as 8700.1, 8710.3C, and 861 0.4F that specifically follow Goodrich in going after rural routes, while totally ignoring mail drops. These orders are illegal insofar as they conflict with documents that are superior, such as regulations or laws, but being illegal doesn't remove the ink from the paper. FAA officials will still cite them when it suits their purpose. The important thing for pilots to understand is that when the Feds cite a document, it doesn't mean they have the law on their side.

For example, there is a direct contradiction between the wording of pilot certificate application form 9710-1, and the wording of the General Aviation Inspectors' Operations Handbook 8700.1 regarding filling out the same form. The effect is that many pilots cannot obey the instructions in the certificate application without violating the requirements found in 8700.1.

Either way the honest pilot responds, he is potentially vulnerable to fines, loss of license, etcetera. This is a perfect example of arbitrary, capricious, and not in accord with law, and a perfect example of what is wrong with the FAA. In this instance, the thing to remember is that the application form is blessed by the administrator per 61.13, and 8700.1 isn't, so the wording in the application prevails. It's just that you may -- or may not -- get an inspector who sees it that way. Again, arbitrary and capricious.

So, fellow pilots, when the FSDO or the examiner says you have to do it because it's in the book, there is a good chance he or she is wrong. You don't have to do it unless the regulations require it, or unless there is a law that says you have to do it.

But; I've gotten ahead of my story again.

### Six Months Earlier...

At Sun 'n Fun in April, I spent half a day at the FAA building trying to resolve the matter, getting handed from person to person and becoming more and more frustrated. I was told that the map requirement was in the FARs. When I asked to see the regulation, the lady searched and finally announced that it wasn't in the regulations, but was in "our (FAA's) laws". I informed her that the FAA doesn't make laws, but she couldn't comprehend the distinction. When I asked to see the map requirement in whatever form it was in, no one could produce that either. I ended up dealing with Mr. Jim Riddle from HQ in Washington. He tried to be helpful, but wasn't.

The only thing I learned for sure at Sun 'n Fun is that there is no shortage of money at FAA. You should see that plush second-story conference room they have. Great place to watch the airshow! Of course, it's empty and unused the other 51 weeks per year. As I sat there looking out at the flightline, I was thinking how nice it would be if FAA Flight Service Stations were allowed to have windows so they could see the airplanes. And the weather.

Ah, but I'm digressing again...

### What Does The Law Say?

I began to do my homework. According to FAA, the reason they needed a map of how to find my rural residence was Public Law 100-690. One thing I learned is that PL 100-690 has almost nothing to do with FAA. Here are some random items from that 1988 law:

•"Authorizes assignment of HHS personnel to work within the organizations and use of traditional native Hawaiian healers as well as Western-trained medical personnel."

•".... Establishes the declared policy of the U.S. Government to create a drug-free America by 1995."

•"Includes provisions to restrict sale or issuance of bank checks, cashier's checks, travelers checks, or money orders for cash in transactions involving more than $3000."

•"Prohibits distribution of obscene matter by cable or subscription television."

•"Requires an OJJDP study of illegal parental abduction of children."

•"Requires DOT rulemaking regarding trucking industry use of emergency flares, and maintenance and inspection of brake systems."

You get the idea. But it gets worse. When I began doing my homework on PL100-690, I wanted to read it. What I just quoted above is from a summary; it's not the actual law itself. I checked with several law libraries and couldn't find a copy of the complete law -- not on paper, not on microfilm, not on computer. I really wanted the entire tome so I could hold it up in court, to compare the part the FAA quoted with the part they didn't quote.

When I got desperate, I called my congressman's office. I know one of the guys there. He went to work on the problem, and learned that when these large bills are passed into law, there are only three copies physically printed:

•One goes to the President. That copy is gone because when an old administration leaves the White House, they take every scrap of paper with them. Each new administration begins with empty bookshelves and clean file cabinets. (Would Ford Motor Corp. or Boeing do that?)

•The second copy of Public Law 100-690 went to the Senate. Nobody could find it.

•The third copy of Public Law 100-690 went to the House, which sent it to the Library of Congress. It is there, but they don't loan it out.

So much for the "public" in Public Law. But the more you

think about it, the more it stinks.

Suppose we had a Senator who was a strong friend of aviation, and suppose he wanted to keep the DEA under control and try to maintain freedom for American citizens who had done nothing wrong. He would have to vote against the "Federal Aviation Administration Drug Enforcement Assistance Act of 1988."

With a title like that, he would be accused at the next election of voting in favor of drugs. Digging deeper, his opponent could show that the Senator had voted in favor of kidnapping and porn. (And against truck flares and Hawaiian healers, too!) What's a poor Senator to do?

### I Never Did Get A Copy Of The Actual Law

But I did find out that the law required FAA to give special attention to pilot certificate applications that use a mailing address that is a post office box or a mail drop. Nothing about rural routes. I vowed to continue the fight.

### Like Pushing on a Rope

In a letter from Mr. Harold Everett, manager of FAA Airmen Certification Branch in OKC written April 24, Everett said, "You may contact the FSDO for another temporary certificate if necessary."

Much later, when I subpoenaed my files, I found that on the very next day, April 25, 1997, the same Mr. Everett sent FAA Form 8060-31(2-91) to the FSDO. The form has a series of boxes that can be checked to make something happen. In this case it's Item 9: "Please provide new temporary certificate to airman and include copy with file".

### The Box was Not Checked

One day this FAA official tells me that I can have a temporary certificate if I ask the FSDO, and the very next day he sends a form to the FSDO indicating that they should not issue it. Thanks, Mr. Everett!

When I called the Nashville FSDO (the district where I had taken the exam and surrendered my certificate), the inspector said that I would have to contact my local FSDO. I did, and was told that they had no paperwork on the matter, and I should contact Airmen Certification Branch (the same Mr. Everett). Round and round we went. There had been an earlier copy of the same form sent to the FSDO back in February; in that case, the box wasn't checked, either. I didn't know anything about it because they don't supply a copy of 8060-31 to the applicant. Perhaps it would spoil their game.

### Delayed, Not Denied?

FAA procedures clearly state that if a certificate application is denied, a certain form will be sent to the applicant. That form gives the applicant the procedures for appeal, and contains a denial number, which will become part of the appeal. In my case, FAA claimed that my application had not been "denied". It had merely been delayed until I provided them with a map. I got the word loud and clear from Ms. Mary Rickey, who works for Mr. Everett. In a phone call, she stated, "If you give us the map you will get your certificate and if you don't, you won't." Period.

Time went by. I called various FAA officials. I talked with FAA lawyers in DC. They had never heard of any requirement for a map. I talked with NTSB lawyers; they had never heard of one either. This was getting curiouser and curiouser.

Then I found a copy of the Federal Register for April 4, 1997. It's about the rewrite of Part 61, and in the lengthy text that explains each change I found some good ammunition. "...61.29... has been revised to incorporate current policy, which is not to accept a post office box as part of a permanent mailing address. " YES!

The FAA rulemongers clearly stated in writing that current FAA policy involves post office boxes. Not a word about rural routes! A few pages later it got even better. The discussion about 61.35 gets directly to the point and talks about Public Law 100-690. Now we're getting somewhere. Again, the requirement is only for post office boxes. Nothing about rural routes.

### Time Out...

Is any of this important to you, dear reader?

I believe it is. Not because you might someday live on a rural route or might rent a post office box. Not even because it demonstrates how screwed up the FAA is. This is important because sooner or later you will be in the position of fighting for your pilot certificate, or fighting for your medical, or fighting a huge fine or other penalty.

If you are going to win, you will have to do your homework.

So a story of how another guy did his homework should give you some idea of how to go about saving your ticket when the time comes. We've read a lot about the pilots who became ensnared in FAA's legal games and lost. If you are going to do better than they did, it's important to compare techniques that lead to success with techniques that lead to failure.

## Going Over the FAA's Head

I wrote the NTSB and requested information on filing an appeal. They sent a fat package containing the laws and rules, together with lots of useful information including sample filled out forms and such. Really a good do-it-yourself kit.

So I filed an appeal (it's called a "petition" in the case of a certificate denial). A docket number was assigned, #CD-33. That's interesting. The "CD" is for Certificate Denial, and 33 is a sequential number beginning in 1958. Just think, in 39 years there have only been 33 pilots, including me, who have fought back. Less than one per year. Why is that?

## Lining Up My Ducks

Then I began in earnest to prepare for the hearing. I subpoenaed my airman file, and everything that FAA might use against my position in this matter. I got copies of the relevant FAA forms and orders. There are more than 1400 currently active FAA orders. Some are a few pages; some weigh many pounds. They should all be available online or on CD-ROM; it would make research incredibly easier. However, less than a half dozen of the 1400 are accessible electronically. That's a shame.

I went to the post office and interviewed the postmaster, and came away with some material that was helpful. It never hurts in a federal matter to have evidence from another federal agency.

I took photos of post office boxes (they probably thought I was crazy) and I took photos of my rural mailbox. Fact is, the old mailbox was beginning to look a little worn, so I installed a shiny new one for the occasion.

About ten days before the hearing I received a phone call from the FAA attorney's office. The lady said (this is a direct quote; I wrote it down as she said it), "We have the materials put together that you subpoenaed, but we can't FedEx to a post office box!"

Clearly the FAA still didn't have a clue as to what this was all about. I wanted to scream, "I don't have a post office box," but I didn't. Instead, I took her statement as a hint of some more evidence I needed: FedEx or UPS items that had been delivered to my residence. I found a couple of shipping labels and an overnight letter.

The photographs were blown up to 8x10 glossies, and they looked great. I explained to the young lady at the one-hour photo counter that these would be evidence in a federal hearing. She seemed very impressed and wished me luck!

The research on Internet didn't take much time, but yielded great results, such as the list of 74 Hispanic pilots who claim to reside in the same suite in Miami. I wasn't sure I could get that evidence admitted; I needed a hook. Judge Mullins lives in Arlington, Texas -- why not look there? Sure enough, I found certificates registered to mail drop addresses in Arlington. That should pique his curiosity. What about Oklahoma City, where the FAA Airmen Certification Branch office is located? Yeah, mail drop certificates there too. I even found pilot certificates using the address of a mail drop company that operates under the name "The Mail Drop"!

### Fool for a Client?

For two days I sat here at the word processor, writing every question I wanted to ask, together with a note of what the answer would be. Hour after hour I arranged and rearranged the sequences. Which witness would I call first? Why? What questions should not be asked? Likewise with the evidence that would be submitted, it was important to build from the ground up, leaving no hole the FAA attorney could use to win on a procedural technicality. That was what scared me the most. I had confidence in my evidence, and I had confidence that my position was proper and legal and just. But that is no protection when the opposition knows a courtroom trick and I don't.

### Did I consider hiring an attorney? No.

There are several reasons, but perhaps the important one is that lawyers don't seem to be winning any aviation cases. Bob Hoover had a couple of the best; Howard Fried had excellent counsel, and so on. Yet they lost. If you are going to lose anyway, why spend the $10,000, $20,000, and more?

When an aviation case comes before the NTSB, it is heard by one of four Administrative Law Judges. NTSB has only four: Judges Pope, Fowler, Geraghty, and Mullins. Aviation attorneys find themselves standing before these same four judges again and again. Worse yet, since both the judges and the attorneys tend to work in one part of the country, an attorney finds himself standing before the same one judge over and over. Now think about it, is that attorney more interested in your one case, or in his many cases overall? He can never pull out all the stops and go for broke; he can never do or say anything that might jeopardize his relationship with this judge.

On the other hand, when you represent yourself, you only have this one case. It is the case. There is no reason to hold back or give it less than all you have. It has been said that a man who represents himself has a fool for a client. Maybe, but that fool and his attorney have interests that are 100% aligned. Plus, the attorney remembers his client's name.

When the FAA is acting illegally (and it often is), all it takes is a lot of homework. It does not take money. It does not take fancy legal talent. It just takes dogged determination to hang on, and hang on, and hang on until you win. That is probably the biggest reason not to hire an attorney. Dogged determination and righteous indignation cannot be rented at xxx dollars per hour. That comes from deep inside.

### D-Day, H-Hour

The day and hour came for the hearing. Judge Mullins was in Oklahoma City for that hearing only. It was held in a real courtroom, with a real, legal stenographer, and a real black robe on His Honor. I've already described how it went. Quick, that's how it went. And it was over. FAA had folded.

Psychologically, I was prepared to lose (I would appeal). I was prepared to win (FAA would appeal). I realized that there might be a legal trick that I couldn't overcome and was as prepared as possible for that. But I was not prepared for the FAA to give up before I got to any of the good stuff. As I sit here two weeks later, writing this at 1:40 a.m., I'm still not prepared for that.

## The Price of Justice

What does it cost to fight the FAA and win? Here is a breakdown:

**Registered mail** $20
**Telephone calls**, very little. Everyone has 800 numbers.
**Color glossies** $70
**Court costs** $0
**Internet time** $0 over what I normally pay
**Mileage to OKC** $90 (300 miles @ .30)
**Copying costs** $100 (1000 pages @ .10)

So that brings it to the $300 range. Or, in pilot terms, three hamburgers.

Of course the big item is my time. On the one hand, you could say that I'm worth X dollars an hour and it cost 300X, or whatever. On the other hand, you could realize that it's September 18 today, and if I hadn't done all that work it would still be September 18 today, so the time doesn't matter.

It's like the story of the salesman driving along the highway. He sees a farmer holding a pig up in an apple tree. Full of curiosity, he turns around and drives back.

"I've just gotta ask, what are you doing?"

"I'm fattening up this pig."

"But won't that take a long, long time?"

"What's time to a pig?"

The NTSB appeal is over and FAA lost. I now have my new certificate, with glider rating, in my wallet. There will be no further appeal. I won.

That is the end of the story. But in the past nine months I've learned some things that might help the next pilot deal with the Feds. On one level this is a story very different from those of Mike Taylor or Howard Fried. On another level, the story is the same. Only the ending is changed.

Fly safely, guys and gals. Just don't confuse flying safe with flying in accord with the FAA.

*...Darryl*

What follows is the complete verbatim transcript of the NTSB hearing before Judge Mullins:

BEFORE THE UNITED STATES OF AMERICA
NATIONAL TRANSPORTATION SAFETY BOARD
Docket No. CD-33
In the Matter of:
ADMINISTRATOR, FEDERAL AVIATION ADMINISTRATION,
Complainant,
V
DARRYL H. PHILLIPS,
Respondent.

The above-entitled matter came on for Hearing, pursuant to Notice, before WILLIAM R. MULLINS, Administrative Law Judge, at Room 1020, 420 West Main, Oklahoma City, Oklahoma, on Friday, September 5, 1997, at 12:30 p.m.
APPEARANCES:
On behalf of the Complainant:
JOSEPH R. STANDELL, ESQ.
On behalf of the Respondent:
DARRYL H. PHILLIPS, Pro Se

INDEX

DIRECT CROSS REDIRECT RECROSS VOIR DIRE
Darryl H. Phillips 15 EXHIBITS

APPELLANT'S IDENTIFIED RECEIVED DESCRIPTION
111-Photographs taken at the Sallisaw United States Post Office.
211-Photographs taken at the Sallisaw United States Post Office.
312-Rental agreement Post Office standard form 1093.
413-Photographs of the mailbox alone.
513-Photographs of mailbox and residence of Mr. Phillips.

PROCEEDINGS

(Time noted: 12:30 p.m.)

JUDGE MULLINS: This is a hearing before the National Transportation Safety Board being held in Oklahoma City.

Today is the 5th day of September of 1997, and this matter is on the petition of Mr. Darryl H. Phillips for the review of the denial of the -- by the Acting Administrator of the Federal Aviation Administration of the issuance of an airman's certificate.
And our Board Docket No. is CD-33.
At this time, and for the record, I would request a statement of appearance by the parties, and I take it, Mr. Phillips, that you're going to be representing yourself in this matter?

THE APPELLANT: That's correct, Your Honor.

JUDGE MULLINS: All right. And for the Administrator?

MR. STANDELL: I'm Joseph R. Standell, S-t-a-n-d-e-l-l.
I'm the Assistant Chief Counsel, c-o-u-n-s-e-l, for the Aeronautical Center, Mike Maroney Aeronautical Center, Federal Aviation Administration, United States Department of Transportation.

JUDGE MULLINS: Thank you.
Now, Mr. Phillips, the trial -- this trial is different than most of the trials that I do, because in this one, you are the Petitioner versus the Administrator, and as the Petitioner, you have the burden of going forward and establishing your evidence by a preponderance of the evidence.
Because you do have that burden, you get to make an opening statement first, you get to close first and last, and you get to put on your evidence first.
But before we go to an opening statement, do you have any preliminary matters that I need to address before the opening?

THE APPELLANT: No, sir.

JUDGE MULLINS: All right. Does the Administrator have anything preliminarily?

MR. STANDELL: Yes, at least one, Your Honor.

We'd like to make a motion to dismiss on jurisdictional grounds. We believe that pleadings have not established and none of the evidence will establish that there has been a denial under Section 44703 here. The pleadings that were shown and the answer that we have submitted to the pleadings show that there was not a denial of an application for an aircraft registration. There is simply a delay in processing to allow Mr. Phillips to comply with the requirements of 6113 and complete the application that's acceptable to the Administrator.

So on that basis, we would move that jurisdictionally, there has been no denial and that the matter is right for dismissal.

THE APPELLANT: Your Honor, I would argue against the granting his motion. The evidence that I will present today will show that I have complied with 6113 and that the Administrator, through the Airman Certification Branch, is operating contrary to the law and operating in a capricious and arbitrary manner.

JUDGE MULLINS: In an abundance of caution, I'm -- I'll just take the motion under advisement and go ahead, since we're here, and receive the evidence because I wouldn't want this matter to go back somewhere if I ruled -- whichever way I ruled -- if ruled for the Administrator and then get reversed, then we'd all have to come back to Oklahoma City.

So I'll just, for the moment, take the motion under advisement and ask that you proceed. And at this time, Mr. Phillips, you may make an opening statement.

THE APPELLANT: Thank you.

MR. STANDELL: May I have -- I have one other preliminary matter?

JUDGE MULLINS: Oh, certainly.

MR. STANDELL: I would just like a clarification with respect to denials, because I'm even less familiar with the precedents than you are, but the question I've got is this: That Mr. Phillips has subpoenaed Mary Rickey and Harold Everett as witnesses, and I assume that he's going to call them.

THE APPELLANT: I will. Those are my two witnesses

MR. STANDELL: Okay. And I understand that Mr. Phillips is not an attorney, and I was wondering if you would clarify for us and clarify for him, in particular, their roles and whether or not he is bound by their testimony, since it's, you know, they have not been established as adverse in any way, that --

THE APPELLANT: No.

MR. STANDELL: -- and I'll take them on cross-examination.

JUDGE MULLINS: Mr. Standell has raised an interesting point, and that is, if you put on these folks that you have subpoenaed in your case in chief, then you may be bound by their testimony, and their testimony may not be favorable to the position you want to put forward here today.

THE APPELLANT: I understand that.

JUDGE MULLINS: At the same time, you know, I've read the pleadings and I'm not sure -- I mean -- well, I think I understand the issue, but I'm not sure why we would need witnesses to support that, other than your own testimony that you submitted this application and it came back with remarks or whatever that would be so indicated.

THE APPELLANT: Your Honor, as I read Section 44703, I see that I have the burden of proof to show that the actions are arbitrary, capricious or not in accord with the law.
In order to do that, I need the testimony of the people that work in the Airman Certification Branch.

JUDGE MULLINS: Well, as I said, you may be bound by what they say. All right. Okay. Then you may proceed with your opening statement.

THE APPELLANT: Thank you, Your Honor.
The specific subject today, whether or not I'm required to submit a map, whether any airman is required to submit a map, is so small as to be almost insignificant. None of us should be here wasting our

time on something that small.

The legal principle behind it is anything but insignificant. What we're really talking about is not a silly map. We're talking about whether the Federal Aviation Administration can violate the spirit and letter of the law set down by Congress, whether they can violate the regulations that FAA has promulgated, whether they can issue orders that are contradictory to other orders, and then pick and choose on any given instance, which they want to enforce and which they want to ignore. Whether they can enforce orders that have expired many years ago, but they're still claiming to enforce them; whether they can operate contrary to law, and that is what this hearing is about today.

Thank you.

JUDGE MULLINS: Do you wish to make an opening statement at this time, Mr. Standell?

MR. STANDELL: Yes, Your Honor, just a brief one, just to correct -- perhaps to correct something that Mr. Phillips has said.

It is not completely true that we required that a map be submitted. We required either that a description of the residence be submitted, or a map, anything that would show where the location of the residence was.

It's our position that the requirement we make is totally consistent with all of the orders, with the basic Statute, 6113, with the application itself, which is very, very clear as to the requirement to submit something in addition to what was submitted here.

So on that basis, we would say that the failure to do so is unjustifiable and is grounds for the stopping of the process, if you would, until he complies.

JUDGE MULLINS: All right. Mr. Phillips, you may call your first witness.

THE APPELLANT: Your Honor, if it please the Court, I have several items of evidence that I would like to enter prior to calling the first witness.

JUDGE MULLINS: All right. If you would, sir, in addition to the numbering system that you might have used, which I -- you know, would be Petitioners 1 or -- I would ask that you put the Board

Docket Number on those, which is CD-33.

THE APPELLANT: okay. If you'll give me just one moment, I'll put it on the first two that I'm going to introduce.

(Whereupon, a discussion was held off the record.)

JUDGE MULLINS: Mr. Standell, if you would just remain seated. We're having a little trouble picking you up here.

MR. STANDELL: Sure.

JUDGE MULLINS: Okay.

THE APPELLANT: Your Honor, the first two photographs that I would like to enter into evidence, which are labeled P-1 and P-2, are photographs taken by me in the past few days at the Sallisaw United States Post Office. P-1 shows a photograph of Post Office boxes (Whereupon, the document was marked for identification as P-1.)

THE APPELLANT: P-2 is -- also shows Post Office boxes, along with a patron that happened by when I was there to take the pictures.

(Whereupon, the document was marked for identification as P-2.)

THE APPELLANT: The reason that I'm showing these is because there is a great deal of confusion on the difference between a Post Office box and a Rural Route.

In preparation for this case, as the Court is aware, I subpoenaed some items from -- or through Mr. Standell, and I received a phone call from a lady who identified herself as being with his office, and I believe her name was Ms. Morgan, although I'm not sure about that.

And she says, "Mr. Phillips, I have the items that you subpoenaed ready," but she says, "We have to have a different address because we cannot Fed Ex to a Post Office Box. Now the point I'm making, Your Honor, is that I don't have a Post Office box.

A Post Office box, as you can see in the pictures, and as we all know, is --

(whereupon, a discussion was held off the record.)

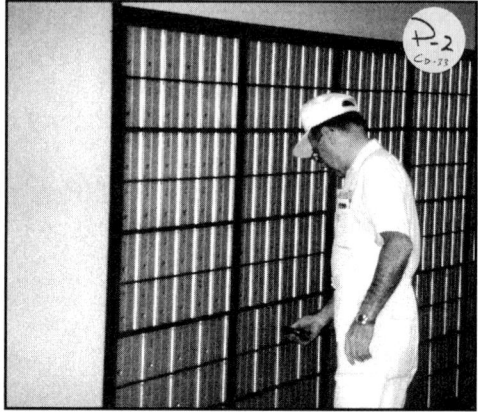

THE APPELLANT: Pat, can you carry the items up there? That would be a lot easier. If you'll give that to his Honor.

The item labeled P-3 is the rental agreement. It is Post Office standard form 1093, which has to do with renting Post Office boxes, which is how you acquire one.

(Whereupon, the document was marked for identification as P-3.)

THE APPELLANT: The next Exhibits, P-4 and P-5 -- give it to the Judge first -- are photographs of my mailbox. P-4 shows the mailbox alone.

Whereupon, the document was marked for identification as P-4.)

THE APPELLANT: P-5 is taken from a different angle. It shows not only the mailbox, but it also shows my residence.

(Whereupon, the document was marked for identification as P-5.)

THE APPELLANT: There is no connection between a Post Office box and a rural mailbox.

The next two items that I would like to put into evidence - here we go are originals of items that we received recently. These happen to be not from Fed Ex. I didn't have anything from Fed Ex. But they happen to be UPS, both overnight and more normal, slow shipment, as evidence of the fact that we do, indeed receive shipments, contrary to what the FAA believed we do get things out in the country the same as people in town do.

I know I'm belaboring this point, but it's important because it goes directly to the heart of this case.

The next thing, Your Honor, that I would like to establish is that my address, which is --

JUDGE MULLINS: Well, you can offer these Exhibits, but if you're going to testify, I'll need to swear you in.

THE APPELLANT: I believe we should do that at this time.

MR. STANDELL: Your Honor, could we have a side bar for one second?

JUDGE MULLINS: Yes.
(Whereupon, a discussion was held off the record.)

MR. STANDELL: I'll withdraw the request for the side bar.

JUDGE MULLINS: All right. Would you stand, sir, and raise your right hand.

Whereupon, DARRYL H. PHILLIPS was called as a witness on behalf of THE APPELLANT, and, having been duly sworn, was examined and testified as follows:

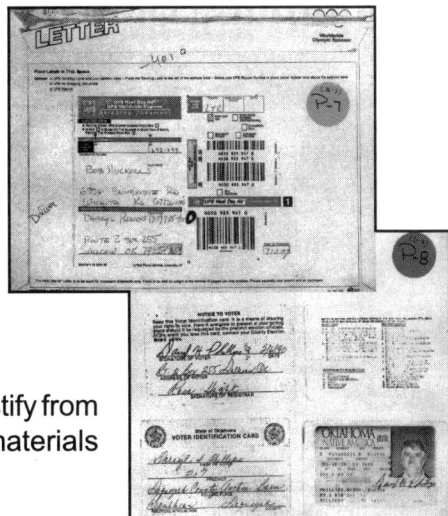

JUDGE MULLINS: I'll let you testify from there so that you have all your materials there, Mr. Phillips.

THE WITNESS: Thank you, sir.

JUDGE MULLINS: Unless counsel has an objection.

MR. STANDELL: No. I have No objection.

JUDGE MULLINS: Okay. Go ahead.

DIRECT EXAMINATION
THE WITNESS: The next item which I would like to enter into evidence, which is labeled P-8 --

JUDGE MULLINS: I've got two labeled P-6.

THE WITNESS: And no P-7?
JUDGE MULLINS: No P-7, and the -- and the two P-6's are exactly the same.

THE WITNESS: Yes. This is 7. Do you have that?

JUDGE MULLINS: No.

THE WITNESS: Okay. One moment, Your Honor.

MR. STANDELL: Your Honor, could I just have a -- perhaps a two-second break, just to confer with Mr. Phillips for just one second?

JUDGE MULLINS: Certainly. Would you like me to step outside?

MR. STANDELL: No. No. That's fine. I just -- one second.
(Whereupon, a discussion was held off the record.)

JUDGE MULLINS: We just had a side bar conference and Mr. Standell has indicated that with the introduction of Petitioner's Exhibit 5, which is a photograph of his residence and his rural route -- post -- mailbox, that the Administrator is satisfied this is sufficient information for them to issue the certificate.
And with that announcement that makes the petition of Mr. Phillips moot, and therefore, the hearing is terminated.

THE WITNESS: Thank you, Your Honor.
(Whereupon, the hearing was adjourned at 1:00 p.m.)

CERTIFICATE
This is to certify that the attached proceedings before the NATIONAL TRANSPORTATION SAFETY BOARD IN THE MATTER OF:
ADMINISTRATOR,
FEDERAL AVIATION ADMINISTRATION, Complainant,
V.
DARRYL H. PHILLIPS, Respondent

DOCKET NUMBER: CD-33
PLACE: Oklahoma City, Oklahoma
DATE: September 5, 1997
were held according to the record, and that this is the original, complete, true and accurate transcript which has been compared to the recording accomplished at the hearing.
Official Reporter

The transcript is complete. At the same time, the transcript is anything but a complete picture of what went on in the courtroom that day.

It is true that FAA attorney Standell used the photograph (exhibit P-5) as the means to end the proceeding. He was going to find some way to stop me from introducing the damning evidence I had against the FAA.

Look at that photograph. Is there anything in it that satisfies the requirement he states in his opening remarks "We required either that a description of the residence be submitted, or a map, anything that would show where the location of the residence was."

Can anyone (other than my neighbors) look at that picture and tell "where the location of the residence was?" Well, there are no palm trees, so I guess that narrows it down a little. Is there anything in that photograph that satisfies the requirement set forth in FAA's Action Notice 8700.2, which states "an airman residing on a rural route must disclose the actual location of his/her residence?? Is there anything in that photograph that satisfies the requirement set forth in FAA's Order 8710.3C, which states "...if the applicant... resides on a rural route, a boat, or in some other location that requires the use of a post office box or rural route number... the applicant must provide the geographical location of the applicant's residence on a separate piece of paper and attest by signature..."? I think any reasonable person would agree that there is nothing in the picture to meet those requirements.

So if FAA says the picture is all they need, that shows (once again) that FAA is not interested in following their own requirements. And if they'll do it on something as small and silly as this, think what they will do when the stakes are higher.

How can the transcript be complete, and simultaneously incomplete? It's those little "sidebar" conversations. That is where much of the real work is done. There is no ticking clock in a transcript, no way to see that the gaps - which look so small on paper - are really larger than the "on the record" proceedings.

Just prior to the point where Standell threw in the towel, there is a ten-minute break where Standell took my two witnesses into the hall for a conversation. I imagine (but don't know) that there must have been some disagreement between them, or it wouldn't have taken so long. He wanted to get this thing stopped. Legally, it is questionable whether he should have been able to take my witnesses (who were only present because I had subpoenaed them) out of the courtroom at all. Indeed, I think a good question could be asked as to whether he could speak with my witnesses at all once the proceeding had begun, even inside the courtroom. But that really doesn't matter; the representative for the Administrator of the FAA was going to find a way to end the proceeding.

Of course they could have ended it earlier. Months earlier, I had explained again and again that what they were requiring was contrary to law. I had explained it in person, and in writing, and on the phone.

They wouldn't listen. They were willing to take me all the way to court in hopes I would knuckle under and give them a silly map.

And the taxpayers paid for it all. It's not just the dollar amount; we should also consider the delays and backups in paperwork processing that had worsened while they were trying to force their illegalities on me. Or look at it this way: Think how much things would be speeded up if they treated all airmen as the law requires. Period.

The lesson? FAA has been winning for a long, long time. It

rarely loses. In fact, FAA loses so rarely that it has lost the muscle tone that only comes from continued exercise. FAA has developed a soft underbelly. As a result, FAA is vulnerable. Federal Anti Aviation has promulgated so many conflicting and contradictory rules that all we airmen have to do is dig in, do our homework, and fight.

At the same time, it is incumbent upon us to not take advantage of this. If you are caught buzzing your girlfriend's house, you should accept your punishment. Better yet, don't do it in the first place. On the other hand, if you and your instructor are practicing forced landings and some country sheriff claims you were below 500 ft AGL, fight like hell.

*As an example of the great weight given to the testimony of people in authority while ignoring much more probative evidence, I offer the following illustration: Several years ago my wife defended a pilot who was accused by a local cop of low flying. The pilot was a local control tower operator who worked part time as a flight instructor for an operator. He had been assigned to fly a photographer to a nearby location to photograph a building. Although the photographer repeatedly requested that he go lower, he repeatedly refused to do so and at the ALJ hearing they both testified to this fact. A local police officer observed the plane and reported it as "flying low." My wife hired an engineer who presented triangulation evidence based on the pictures themselves demonstrating that the airplane was over twelve hundred feet AGL. In spite of all this, the ALJ accepted the guesswork of the cop as to the height of the airplane, on the basis that as experienced law officer ought to know what he's saying! The pilot suffered a thirty-day suspension.*

The rules are supposed to support the goals of safety and efficiency. It's up to us, each one of us, to hold the FAA to that standard.
-- Darryl Phillips

---------------------------------------------------------------------

The foregoing transcript and Darryl's comments were published on the Internet (on America OnLine). What follows are selected comments received in response to Darryl's story. Three of the people who commented said the fight was foolish and Darryl should have simply given the FAA a map, but the majority of comments were overwhelmingly supportive. The limitation of space only permitted the publication here of a few of the many comments received.

(1) Thanks for the greater insight into the FAA. I once had a similar experience. During the FAA "hearing", Judge Fowler nodded off while my attorney was speaking (you think maybe the judge had already made up his mind?) and my attorney felt it was unnecessary to disturb him by waking him.

*(1a) Darryl's answer*
*Sorry to hear about Judge Fowler. The only one I know is Judge Mullins, and I was very favorably impressed by him. If all judges were as good, we would have a better justice system.*

*Darryl*

(2) Way to go, Darryl! You've set a great example. Again, nice work with the FAA....

(3) To: Darryl Phillips
From: Mike Taylor-
Darryl, I commend you on your success. I certainly could have been more prepared for my hearing if I knew the FAA would lie about telephone conversation, fabricate and misrepresent info as well as totally rule out FAR 61.41, which had been explained to me by the same FSDO a month before, that it did apply to this training. Also that info was supported by other inspectors in the SDL FSDO. However, Inspector DeMartini and FAA Attorney Tsuda were given that info and decided to pursue the case anyway. Finally, regarding ALJ, I should have known the interest my case had to Judge Geraughty from his very first comment (off the record of course) "DOES ANYONE KNOW WHERE THE "O" CLUB IS ON MCAS YUMA". I lay awake reliving the nightmare analyzing why the FAA did what they did and how Geraughty prevented my attorney from getting info in the record.
One attorney I spoke with before he knew about my experience described Judge Geraughty's hearing process as follows. He will allow FAA fairy tales for hours building a case, then about 4:00

PM he will say that's enough, regardless the stage of the hearing. Remember he either has a plane to catch or an appointment at the "O" club. (The "O" Club is my observation).

You seemed to have been prepared for the "Unethicity" of the FAA. I was not.

(4) Hi, This is a terrible commentary on a federal agency that is here to "help you".

(5) I can't help but think of the definition of bureaucrat from **The American College Dictionary**: 1. an official of a bureaucracy. 2. an official who works by fixed routine without exercising intelligent judgment. I'm sure Darryl saw this in his endeavors.

(6) I have lived at 10 different Rural Routes since the day I was certificated A&P, IA, and Private Pilot, and have drawn 10 maps (Three in Oklahoma) to my house and one to my hangar (which was located on a public airport in Oklahoma, but happened to have a Rural Route address [perhaps I could have photo copied an airport facility directory]). I solved the problem by moving to rural Kansas (but of course that's not why I moved) where we have addresses like town folk even way out in the boondocks; they call them 911 addresses. But unless you work in the post office I doubt you could find 15 NW 20 Avenue. But it made them happy.

(7) The proverbial little guy wins! I am not surprised the FAA can make a mistake. I do continue to wonder at the mentality that makes government agencies so reluctant to say "I MADE A MISTAKE".

(8) As a new pilot, some personal experiences as well as reading about other pilots' experiences has helped temper my idealism about aviation and the FAA. The realization that the FAA is at least as unethical and unreasonable as any other federal
"civil servants" (ha!) seem to think that their job description involves making life difficult for their customers, for no good reason.

(9) He should have just sent them the map. The FAA is not my best friend but to fight it out over something this small is not a good use of time or effort. All we got out of this case is one happy warrior, and a

lot of pissed off FAA types. Who, by the way, will probably take it out on the next poor fool looking for some simple common sense.

(10) So your recommendation to others who have been insulted, abused and unfairly treated by those obsequious FAA employees is to shut up, and quietly do as you are told? And do it because of fear of retribution.

Tell me, what is the point of having Federal Regulations, if a secret policy manual memo has the force of law? Where is JUSTICE? Hiding under the table, hoping that the Feds will pick on somebody else?

Your intimidation and fearful compliance with any FAA demand, no matter how unfair or unreasonable, serves to embolden these bureaucrats. If yours is the prevailing opinion among American citizen pilots, I saddened beyond my ability to express it.

Let us continue to applaud those with the courage to stand and fight.

(11) From Darryl Phillips

*I agree completely that the item (a map) is small. The map itself is insignificant.*

*But the rule of law is not insignificant. The rule of law is all that stands between us and tyranny or anarchy, and the FAA is bent on destroying the rule of law. That is one point. But there are other points also. I would have been much happier to have been fighting Mike Taylor's case; it is a thousand times more important to aviation than a silly map. However, we have a legal system where I am precluded from fighting his battle. I have no standing in that court proceeding. Likewise, Mike could not fight Howard's battle; Mike and Howard could not fight Bob Hoover's; and none of us will be able to help fight your battle when your time comes.*

*It's unfortunate, but that is the way our judicial system works. I didn't see the map thing coming, I didn't choose that fight, but when the situation happened all I could do was remember Bob Hoover and all the others, and fight like crazy. Another point: FAA cloaks everything in the veil of "safety", and aviation has not yet learned how to pierce that veil. (We gotta learn that.) But in the case of the map, the subject was not safety. It was "The Drug War" and FAA did not hold the high moral ground. We did.*

*It was an opportunity to demonstrate that FAA is only a bully, not a responsible organization. Too good an opportunity to let pass.*

*Perhaps my case will form the basis for a lawsuit in federal court, which (when won) could form the basis for questioning FAA actions in aviation cases that are more important than a silly map.*

*Darryl*

Darryl won his point, but did he really win the war? In the next chapter we will take a look at what never made it into the public record and what would serve to demonstrate just how the FAA operates in the exercise of power that they really don't have.

# Chapter 4

# Darryl Wins But the Aviation Community Loses

When the FAA attorney folded and agreed to let Darryl Phillips have his certificate with the new rating, Darryl had won the case and made his point. But what did he really win?

All the work he had put in and all the research he had done -- all that careful preparation -- was intended to show just how the FAA ignored the law and disregards its own rules when it suits them to do so. None of this proof, however, made it into the record.

Darryl has graciously provided me with the notes he had prepared for the trial, along with the exhibits he had intended to offer. I have a *Juris Doctor* degree and many years ago I passed the Michigan bar, although I have never practiced law.

I have spent countless hours in court testifying as an expert witness on matters aeronautical. And if there is anything I have learned it is that the key to winning in court is to, like the Boy Scouts, **be prepared**. The thoroughness with which Darryl Phillips prepared his case can only be described as outstanding.

Once again, the only way to adequately express this is in Darryl's own words. Please bear in mind that these notes were prepared before the hearing and are not a transcript of the hearing itself. For that, see Chapter 3. He carefully wrote out the questions he intended to ask his witnesses and here they are:

**List of Exhibits to be submitted by Petitioner -**
NTSB Hearing - Docket CD-33/5 September 1997/Judge Mullins

**P-1** Original color photo of post office boxes taken by Petitioner at the

Sallisaw OK Post Office

**P-2** Original color photo of post office boxes and a patron, taken by Petitioner at the Sallisaw, OK Post Office

**P-3** Original Postal Service Form 1093 - Post office box rental agreement - supplied to Petitioner by Sallisaw Postmaster

**P-4** Original color photo of mailbox belonging to Petitioner

**P-5** Original color photo of mailbox and residence belonging to Petitioner

**P-6** Original J.C. Penney address label, shipment via UPS to Petitioner's residence

**P-7** Original UPS next-day air letter to Petitioner's residence

**P-8** Photocopy of Petitioner's Oklahoma driver's license and Oklahoma voter registration card

**P-9** Certified True Copy of the complete airman file pertaining to Petitioner

**P-10** Certified True Copy of the complete application for glider rating by Petitioner

**P-11** Photocopies of pages 16243, 16245, 16306, and 16308 of the Federal Register Vol 62, No 65, Friday April 4, 1997

**P-12** Photocopy of FAA Form 8710-1 (7-95)

**P-13** Photocopy of FAA Order 8700.2 dated 18 August 1989

**P-14** Original document comparing Airman Database with Mail Drop addresses

********

## Strategy for NTSB Hearing - 5 Sept 1997

Establish that I am the Petitioner, and state the purpose of the hearing.

How to do that:

1...Introduce myself

2...The specific subject of the hearing (whether FAA can require a map) borders on the insignificant, but the purpose of the hearing goes to the heart of the rule of law and is therefore very significant indeed. This court is being asked to decide whether the FAA must follow the precepts set forth in law and in regulation, or whether elements within the FAA are free to ignore the Code of Federal Regulations; free to enforce orders which expired many years ago; and free to make up and enforce policies which are contradictory, arbitrary, capricious; and free to operate in a way that is contrary to law.

## Establish difference between a Post Office Box and a Rural Mailbox.

How to do that:
1...Enter into evidence photos of Post Office Boxes. (P-1, P-2)

2...Enter into evidence copy of rental document from Post Office. (P-3)

3...Enter into evidence photos of my mailbox. (P-4, P-5)

4...Describe:
       •PO Boxes are rented, mailboxes are owned

       •PO Boxes are located at the Post Office (no one lives there), while mailboxes are located at the residence where the addressee lives exhibits (P-6, P-7)

5...Enter into evidence two UPS items sent to Rt. 2 Box 255.

Tell what FAA said: *"We cannot FedEx to a Post Office Box"* (Ms. Morgan, 4:25 PM, August 25, 1997).

Describe that FedEx, UPS, and the others regularly deliver to rural addresses, and the error is in FAA's lack of distinction between the two. People who live in the country are not second-class citizens.

**Show that Rt. 2, Box 255 is my permanent address**

How to do that:
1...Enter into evidence copy of Oklahoma Driver's License and P-8

**Oklahoma Voter Identification Card**
2...Note that the Oklahoma Voter Identification Card is dated 6 February 1990, which is evidence of the same address for at least the past 7 years.

3...Note that the Oklahoma Voter Identification Card uses the location (Rt.2 Box 255) to determine a precinct (307). Rt. 2 Box 255 is more than a mailing address; it is a location.

**Introduce exhibits P-9, P-10**
4...Enter into evidence Certified True Copies of FAA files. Compare 1988 Airman's Certificate with 1996 Airman Certificate application, and show that the address has been the same for the past 8 years.
Show that Airmen Certification actions are not according to law.

**How to do that:**
1...Introduce the portion of PL 100-690 provided by Mr. Standell in response to the subpoena. The law is crystal clear, it cites post office box and mail drop.
It does not say, nor imply or suggest, that any other sort of mailing address is involved. We only have one law to consider here, and PL 100-690 is it. I have already demonstrated that my address is neither a post office box

nor a mail drop, and is therefore not subject to this law. Regulations. Such are issued by various governmental departments to carry out the intent of the law. Agencies issue regulations to guide the activity of those regulated by the agency and of their own employees and to ensure uniform application of the law." (Black's Law Dictionary, 6 ed, page 1286)

**So let us examine the regulations FAA has provided:**
2...Introduce 14 CFR 61.13(a). It states "An applicant for an airman certificate, rating, or authorization under this part must make that application on a form and in a manner acceptable to the Administrator." At the time of my original application in December, 1996, this was the only applicable regulation. I will get to the "form and manner" shortly. But now there are two more regulations that shed light on the subject, which became effective on August 4:

**Exhibit P-11**
3...Enter into evidence Federal Register Vol 62, No. 65, / Friday, April 4, 1997, pages 16243, 16245, 16306, and 16308, with the pertinent parts highlighted.
On page 16243 col 2: "In the final rule, paragraph (d)(2) has been revised to incorporate current policy, which is not to accept a post office box as part of a  permanent mailing address." This is a clear statement from FAA headquarters in Washington DC that current policy involves post office boxes, not rural routes.
On page 16306 col 3 is the exact wording of 14 CFR 61.29(d)(2) "The permanent mailing address (including ZIP code), or if the permanent mailing address includes a post office box number, then the person's current residential address;" There is no mention of maps, no mention of rural routes, only the requirement for the applicant to supply his or her actual residential address.
On page 16245 col 2 is a more extensive comment from FAA in Washington that goes directly to the subject: "In the proposed paragraph (a)(2), the current requirements for the presentation of personal identification found in FAA Order

8700.1, "General Aviation Operations Inspector's Handbook," were included and clarified. These identification procedures were established in response to the Drug Enforcement Assistance Act of 1988 (Pub. L. 100-690, November 18, 1988).

The proposal required an applicant to present identification consisting of the applicant's photograph, signature, and date of birth showing that the applicant meets or will meet the age requirements for the certificate sought before the expiration date of the knowledge test report. The proposal would also require an applicant to present identification containing his or her actual residential address, if different from the applicant's mailing address....."

On page 16308 col 3 is the paragraph referred above: "(iv) Actual residential address, if different from the applicant's mailing address." Note that there is no mention of rural routes nor post office boxes, only the requirement that the applicant supply the address where he or she actually resides. Since no one physically resides inside a post office box or a mail drop, this section is in accord with both the spirit and letter of PL 100-690.

Note that in each instance, the requirement is for an address, not for a "location of the residence", which the Airmen Certification Branch is attempting to require. This attempt is clearly not according to law, and not in accord with the regulations.

3...Going back to 14 CFR 61.13(a). "An applicant for an airman certificate, rating, or authorization under this part must make that application on a form and in a manner acceptable to the Administrator."

4...Call Mr. Harold Everett to testify.

• Describe your position, duties, and length of service. (Establish that he is qualified to answer questions regarding Airmen Certification Branch procedures)

• Describe the chain of command, both up and down.

(Demonstrate that he is below DC and carries out policy as opposed to making policy)

• Enter into evidence FAA Form 8710-1 (7-95). P-12

• Are you familiar with this form?

• Do you process a lot of this form?

• Describe for the Court what a blank form looks like. (two sheets bound together)

• Do you accept handwritten applications on plain tablet paper or anything like that, or is form 8710-1 the only currently acceptable form to apply for an airman certificate?

• Is this the form referred to in 61.13?

• So you agree that this form is acceptable to the Administrator?

• When was it last revised? (July '95)

• When was it previously revised before that? (Prompt if necessary: July '92)

• Would you please read the title of the instruction page?

• If the form is acceptable to the Administrator, and there are detailed instructions that are an integral part of the form, would you agree that those instructions are acceptable to the Administrator? (If answer is no, get into questions about who works for whom, about who makes policy, and about the definition of arbitrary and capricious) But assuming the answer is yes:

• Please read for the Court the instructions that are acceptable to the Administrator regarding mailing address. That is Block E.

• Do you agree that if the form acceptable to the Administrator contains specific and detailed instructions such as these, it constitutes "a manner acceptable to the Administrator"? (If no, go back and explore his determination to undermine the authority of the Administrator.) If yes:

• Do you agree that FAA policy requires that an applicant use his permanent mailing address? (If no, go back and repeat above with different phrasing, looking for the point where Everett and Administrator part company. Then get back into arbitrary and capricious) If yes:

• So justification must be provided only when something else is used in place of the permanent address?

• Do you recognize this letter dated 24 April 1997? (4/24 FAA letter to me in airman file)

• Would you please describe the letter to the Court?

• Did you sign it? (Explore who wrote it, who approved it, etc.)

• Now that you have had time to study this matter further, are there any statements in this letter that you feel are in error or need clarification?
(Give him a chance!)

• Enter into evidence 8700.2 (P-13)

• Is this the document you were referring to in the letter of 24 April?

• Would you read for the Court the date 8700.2 issued? (18 Aug 89)

• Would you read for the Court the date 8700.2 expired? (18 Aug 90)

• How many years have passed since this order expired?

• What is the purpose of an expiration date on a document?

- Is it the usual policy of the Airmen Certification Branch to enforce orders or procedures that have expired many years ago, or is this particular document being treated differently? (goes to arbitrary and capricious)

- Did you know that 8700.2 was expired when you cited it in your 24 April letter? (Yes or no, gotcha!)

- Please read for the Court the first line of the third paragraph of your letter. ("FAA Form 8710-1, Airman Certificate and/or Rating Application, has not been revised,")

- Mr. Everett, is that a true statement? You testified above that the current revision is 7-95 and the previous one was 7-92, so in truth the form as been revised at least twice since August of 1989. Is that not so? (Play it by ear here. This goes to something more serious than arbitrary and capricious; it is downright deception. If he takes the tack that the form was revised but this part wasn't, it's back to Everett trying to overrule the Administrator as to what should and should not be in the application form, i.e., placing himself above the Administrator in making policy.)

- Please read for the Court the last sentence on page one. ("You may contact the FSDO for another temporary certificate if necessary.")

- Please refer to form 8060-31, dated 2/20/97, (contained in the application file) sent from your office to the Nashville Flight Standards District Office.
Please read item 9 for the Court. (9. District Office: Please provide new temporary certificate to airman and include copy with file.)

- Mr. Everett, is that item checked? (No)

- Now please refer to the copy of 8060-31 dated 4/25/97. Was item 9 checked there? (No)

• Are you aware that the Flight Standards District Office will not issue a temporary certificate unless they are directed to do so? A simple checkmark from your office is all it would have taken to prevent me from being grounded.
You had two opportunities to grant me a new temporary certificate, and you chose not to.

• Refer back to the 2/20/97 copy of 8060-31. Please read for the Court the typed message from your office to the Nashville Flight Standards District Office in item 10. (Please submit physical address or map of location of applicant's physical location. See Order 8700.1, Vol. 2, Chapter 1, page 1-18.)

• Can you explain to the Court why you cite one standard when communicating with the FSDO, and a completely different standard when communicating with the applicant?

•Does this not strike you as arbitrary and capricious?

• Based on the content of my files which are certified to be true and complete, can you tell the Court whether or not I currently hold a valid pilot certificate and what date it was issued?

• Having studied my application in preparation for this hearing, other than the question of residential address, are you aware of any reason why the glider aero-tow rating should not be issued?

• Thank you, Mr. Everett. I have no more questions at this time.

Show that Airmen Certification actions are arbitrary and capricious.

6...Call Mary Rickey to testify

• Do you prefer Ms., Mrs., Miss? (make her more comfortable)

• Describe your position, duties, and length of service. (establish that she is qualified to answer questions regarding Airmen Certification Branch procedures)

- What are the two addresses that are cited in the law? (P.O. Boxes and Mail Drops)

- We know what a post office box is. What is a mail drop?

- In your capacity in the Airmen Certification Branch, can you tell the Court what has been done since 1988 to comply with the law regarding mail drops?

- Enter into evidence database information document P-14.

- If you received an application for a pilot certificate with the address 835 E. Lamar Boulevard #120, Arlington, Texas 76011, would that address cause you to reject the application?

- Are you aware that you have issued pilot certificates to persons using mail drops right here in Oklahoma City, the city where the Airmen Certification Branch is located?

- Are you aware of a company with 2600 franchise locations across the United States called Mail Boxes Etc? This is a mail drop. In Miami, Florida, a known center for illegal drug trade, I easily found 23 pilot certificates with mail drop addresses.

- Are you aware that you have issued pilot certificates to 74 men with Hispanic names who all claim to live in the same apartment in Miami?

- Ms. Rickey, what is the meaning of the phrase, "Post Office address?"

- Referring to form 8710-1 in my application file, Designated Examiner's Report, please explain to the Court the meaning of the boxes that the examiner checked.

- Having studied my application in preparation for this hearing, other than the question of residential address, are you aware of any reason why the glider aero-tow rating should not be issued?

● Thank you, Ms. Rickey. I have no further questions at this time.

Show that I have met all qualifications to hold the glider rating.

How to do that:

1...The application has been bounced back to the FSDO twice, and no problem other than the address has been cited.

2...The application form is properly filled out, and properly signed by the Instructor, by the Designated Examiner, and by the FSDO Inspector.

3...Mr. Everett found no reason to reject or deny.

4...Ms. Rickey found no reason to reject or deny.

5...In a telephone call with Ms. Rickey, she stated, "If you give us the map you will get the certificate, and if you don't, you won't." This clearly indicates that there is no other reason to deny.

### Closing Statement
Make closing statement asking Judge to find in my favor, and requesting a written decision that will be understandable to the full Board and if necessary to the Federal Court.

### Hopscotch
August 18, 89....Order 8700.2 says "The airman applications will be revised to provide for this disclosure and the separate statement will only be used as an interim procedure".

March 1, 1992....8700.1 vol 2 chap 1 sec 4 para 5(B)(2) says "Once FAA Form 8710-1 has been revised, this separate disclosure will no longer be necessary."

July 1992....Form 8710-1 is revised and approved by the

Administrator, but the language regarding permanent address does not change.

July 1995....Form 8710-1 is revised and approved by the Administrator again, but the language again does not change.

February 27, 1997....8700.1 Chg 14 chap 5 sec 2 para 5(D) says: "Compare the Identification with the personal information provided on FAA Form 8710-1. (See Volume 2, chapter 1, Section 4, paragraph 5.)"

In other words, it does not matter that the application form has been revised and revised again, approved each time by the Administrator in accord with the law and the regulations. There are people in the FAA at lower levels than the Administrator who are determined to thwart the will of the Administrator and do it however they please.

............................................................................................

How's that for thorough preparation? It is such a classic example that it ought to be published and used as a text in the Trial Practice courses in Law Schools all around the country!

Darryl certainly had his ducks all lined up. Unfortunately, he never got the opportunity to make public the stupidity of the bureaucratic system and the differential manner in which individual bureaucrats treat various members of the public.

No wonder the FAA attorney capitulated when he did. He did succeed in keeping this stuff from getting out into the public records where it could jump up and bite the FAA in future legal actions.

Thus, although Darryl Phillips won in the sense that forced the agency to give him his certificate without having to provide the demanded map, in the larger sense we all lost because the attempt to demonstrate the unlawful actions of the FAA was thwarted.

**PART 4
DECISIONS AND OPINIONS**

Now we're ready to look at how the regulations of the United States Code of regulations Title 14, The Federal Air Regulations, are interpreted by those who really count, the Administrative Law Judges, the National Transportation Safety Board, and the United Stated Courts of Appeals. In the English legal system, which is followed here in the United States, there are two kinds of law; Statutory law, which is enacted by appropriate authority (Congress, state legislatures, city counsels, etc.) and written down, and "bench-made law", that which is determined by the judiciary through their interpretations of the statutes, ordinances, regulations and precedents. Once a court with appropriate authority has rendered a decision interpreting a rule, that decision acts as a precedent in guiding future actions involving the same set of facts as they relate to the same situation. This means that the task of the defendant airman is to differentiate the facts in his particular case from those on which the precedent rests. In the case of FAA enforcement actions, an ALJ's decision, if it goes unchallenged and unreversed by higher authority (the NTSB or the Court of Appeals), and so on up the line, thus becomes the law of the land as far as the aviation community is concerned.

# Chapter 5

# OK, So What Now?

## The First Step

Now that we've seen the viciousness with which the agency pursues violations, what can we, as airpersons, do to avoid becoming victimized by this implacable system? Obviously, if we never commit a violation, they will have no excuse to go after us, but that is not only difficult, it is nigh to impossible. Next time you are driving an automobile, see just how far you can travel without committing an act that could get you a traffic ticket if a patrolman caught you. Then, next time you are flying an airplane see if you can recognize anything you have done that could be construed as a violation. Add to this the large number of violations that we can commit without even being aware of having done so -- and remember, we don't have to actually commit a violation to be charged with having done so. An inspector only has to suspect that we **might** have done something contrary to the regulations as he sees them.

Even if we are successful in remaining in full compliance, there is no guarantee that some inspector will not twist a regulation so as to interpret it to suit his purpose, as evidenced by the Taylor case and countless others as well as my own. It therefore behooves us to know just what steps we must take to defend ourselves in the event that we should receive a Letter of Investigation. As demonstrated on the Violation Flow Chart (Figure 1), these steps range from the informal meeting with the investigating inspector and an FAA Associate Counsel all the way to the US Circuit Court of Appeals (and perhaps even to the Supreme Court). However, before we get into this we must revisit the NASA Aviation Safety Reporting System (the NASA ASRS form).

## The ASRS Report

Every airperson should have a supply of the NASA Aviation Safety Reporting Forms in his/her flight bag! Air carrier crewmembers file these reports regularly and frequently, and the general aviation pilot should too. The forms are available at all FAA facilities (Flight Service Stations and Flight Standards District Offices). There is only one problem that I see in following this procedure. This is in the fact that, frequently, airpeople unknowingly blunder into committing violations; in which case, there would be no occasion to realize that filing a report would be appropriate. By the time that the affected individual becomes aware that she/he is being investigated, the time limit for filing has long past. Otherwise, if one even suspects that s/he might be involved in a violation investigation, a report should be filed. To avoid the sanction attendant on a violation, the report **must** be filed within the ten-day window between the occurrence and the filing. The burden of proving that the report was mailed timely is on the airperson, so it behooves him or her to file the report by certified mail, return receipt requested, even though the normal procedure is for NASA to send the reporter a date-stamped reply testifying that the report was received on a given date.

Back in Chapter One, I explained how the NASA ASRS system works, but let me go into a bit more detail here. Bear in mind that in order for an ASRS report to protect an airman from the sanction resulting from a violation, the violation must be **inadvertent** rather than deliberate. If, for example, a pilot's transponder encoder, although certified within tolerance, should be right at the edge of the tolerance, and his altimeter, also certified within tolerance, should also be right at the edge of the allowance, and ATC should report the pilot for an altitude bust, s/he could claim that it was inadvertent. If a controller's instructions were not crystal clear and the airperson blundered into airspace where he or she didn't belong, it might be considered inadvertent.

In addition to deliberate actions constituting flight violations, the factors that will prevent filing an ASRS report from protecting one from sanction are: one, criminal activity; and two, accidents involving death, serious injury, or substantial aircraft damage as defined by the FAA (in fact right on the reporting form it says in bold print **"DO NOT REPORT AIRCRAFT ACCIDENTS AND CRIMINAL ACTIVITY ON THIS FORM"**). Finally, incidents revealing a lack of competency or qualifications of the airman to hold a certificate of the grade held (as demonstrated on a "609 ride").

If more than one individual should be involved in a single incident, each should file a separate report to protect him/herself. Since the program was established to provide an incentive for airpeople to report unsafe incidents and conditions, immunity from sanction is provided to the reporter, and confidentiality is guaranteed. As soon as NASA receives a report, it is deidentified and assigned a number, thus assuring confidentiality for the reporter. Neither the FAA nor anyone else has access to the identity of the reporter.

In spite of Darryl Phillips heroic and successful effort to beat the system, few of us have the time to devote to the monumental job of research he undertook. Therefore, the first step after receiving an LOI should be to retain the services of a knowledgeable attorney who specializes in aviation matters, particularly violation cases. Just any old trial lawyer won't do. Most trial lawyers are used to playing by the rules, but when dealing with the FAA, the rules go out the window and are subject to change without notice. Only an attorney used to dealing with this system is able to follow the fancy footwork of the inspectors and attorneys who work for the agency, as they twist and turn in their efforts to nail a frequently innocent airperson with the maximum penalty possible. They do all this in the name of safety, often when there is no safety issue whatever involved. It has been said that the FAA creates what they call a safety issue and then, to make themselves look good, they rush to the rescue by creating a new -- and useless -- regulation. They then charge one or more airmen with violating this and perhaps several other regulations. Makes them look like they are taking positive action, doesn't it? The agency serves up this pap to satisfy the public; if it does nothing else, it does make for good public relations.

When an airman receives a LOI, s/he must consider himself a suspect, and the investigating inspector a policeman, and when an FAA attorney gets into the act, he is a prosecutor. If the airperson or his attorney should decide to respond to the Letter of Investigation, he or she must be very careful to say nothing that in the wildest imagination of the inspector or the FAA attorney could possibly be construed as an admission of wrongdoing. Even so, the Friendly Feds might find a way to twist a harmless remark into an admission. In other words, don't merely be very careful; be very, very careful! If you are not, whatever you say might very well come back to haunt you.

If the airman has a good attorney who can successfully spar with the FAA lawyer without giving anything away, and/or if the airman can keep his cool while dealing with these people who are likely to make simply outrageous statements in an attempt to elicit a damaging response, it is a good idea to go for an informal conference. This gives the victim an opportunity to feel out the other side and see just what they have and what they are looking for. Also, if a reasonable compromise is offered (quite unlikely - when has the FAA ever been reasonable?), and the airman is actually guilty of **something**, it might be well to settle the matter right there. The key here is to play this meeting in such a way as to appear to desire to cooperate without giving away anything.

In many cases, any effort at cooperation is taken as a sign of weakness, and the people who represent the agency will just bore in harder. If this appears to be the case, the airman had better be prepared to play hardball and become just as pugnacious as the other side, still being very careful to not give anything away. By hardball, I mean the airperson or his lawyer should take off the gloves and get tough. He should stand fast on his rights, if the FAA is willing to admit that he has any rights.

Throughout the meeting, the airperson should be polite but firm. If and when it becomes obvious that it is going nowhere, it is time to clam up and say nothing at all. Just announce that you want a hearing before a NTSB Administrative Law Judge.

Of course, if you have the time to do so, you can represent yourself as Darryl Phillips did. This will take a monumental job of research and preparation. It is axiomatic that the side that does the best job of preparing its case wins lawsuits.

The attorney (in this case the client who represents himself) who does his homework and comes prepared is very likely to prevail over the lawyer who treats his case as a routine matter and doesn't bother to come thoroughly prepared. In the last chapter you saw how Darryl had prepared, even to the extent of writing out the questions he intended to ask his witnesses. Another unique feature of the Phillips case is the fact that in this instance the airman was the plaintiff, suing the government, rather than being in the position of having to defend himself against the agency. It is generally easier to be a defendant than a plaintiff because the burden falls on the plaintiff to prove his case.

## The Next Step

It is at the hearing before the NTSB Administrative Law Judge that all that work of research and preparation pays off. The airperson has the right to subpoena witnesses and documents and present evidence. He also has the right to cross-examine the FAA's witnesses, presupposing the ALJ will allow him to do so, as Judge Geraghty did not in the Taylor case. Unfortunately, Taylor's attorney wasn't used to dealing with the FAA. He made the mistake of assuming that he was dealing with reasonable and honorable people -- which neither the FAA inspector who testified nor the FAA attorney who increased the penalty in midstream appears to be.

The ALJs, like the old-time Circuit Judges, actually travel a circuit and how the hearing goes will depend in large measure on just which area of the country the airperson lives. There is one of these Administrative Law Judges employed by the NTSB who is a reasonable individual and who will fairly evaluate the evidence.

I am referring to Judge W. Roger Mullins, who is a pilot. Unlike Judge Geraghty in the Taylor case, who cut off the defense attorney without giving him the opportunity to question Inspector DeMartini as to how he determined that Taylor had not given his student adequate training, I believe that Judge Mullins would no doubt have admitted this line of questioning.

It must be understood that, although it has all the appearance of a regular law court, unlike a law court, an administrative tribunal is not bound by the conventional rules of evidence and the ALJ can admit (or exclude) just about anything he chooses. Unless he clearly abuses his authority or his rulings are clearly against the great weight of the evidence, he is not likely to be overruled by the NTSB.

In more than one case (not my own), I have personally seen

Judge Fowler take mitigating circumstances into account and reduce FAA proposed penalties by a substantial amount. In one case, he knocked down a proposed suspension from sixty days to ten days, and then picked a ten-day period during which the affected pilot had not flown.

On the whole, however, the ALJs, with the exception of Mullins, almost act as a rubber stamp, giving the FAA whatever it asks for. Other than Mullins, these guys know almost nothing about aviation and are inclined to give great weight to whatever the investigating inspector has to say. The really unfortunate thing about this entire system is that the cards are stacked heavily against the airperson. Unless the airman or his/her attorney can make it impossible to prove that the airperson did whatever he/she is charged with, he or she is likely to lose.

By making its proofs, I mean the government has to actually place the airman in the airplane at the time of the occurrence, and unless s/he admits he was flying the airplane at the time, the FAA will have a difficult time proving that that specific individual committed the violation. That's why it is so important to give away nothing. Make 'em prove it!

### The Final Administrative Step

If the airperson loses at the ALJ hearing, or if the FAA appeals, the final step in the administrative process is the NTSB hearing. Unfortunately, here again, the cards are stacked in favor of the government. The Board is most reluctant to overturn its own ALJ who has already ruled against the airman and in favor of the FAA. As is the case in any appeal-level hearing, the only issue, or issues, that may be considered is (are) whether the lower court (in this case the ALJ) committed an error of law in the conduct of his hearing. And such an error must be clearly demonstrated for the airperson to prevail. An example would be if the judge simply ignores a rule of the Board in making his decision.

At this level no new evidence may be presented, other than that which was brought before the ALJ. As is the case in any appellate situation, the entire NTSB hearing is on the basis of the record made at the ALJ hearing, so it is imperative for the airman to get all his evidence in at that level. This is where all that homework and preparation comes into play, and make no mistake, the side that is best prepared is the side that is most likely to prevail! This fact simply cannot be overemphasized. The airman's attorney just has to be better prepared than the FAA attorney is, and in this preparation, the airperson must be ready to assist his lawyer with research. Of course, if he or she acts in *pro se*, he has it all to do.

Finally, it must be remembered that since the members of the Board are appointed (they are political appointees), they are very likely to be responsive to public opinion and to the federal administration that appointed them.

### The United States Circuit Court of Appeals

After all the administrative remedies are exhausted, a violation case may be taken to the federal court system at the level of the US Circuit Court of Appeals (See the Enforcement Flow Chart - Figure 1). Here again, we are dealing with an appeal situation and only those matters that are on the record made at the lower levels may be considered. No evidence is admitted and only a clear error in applying the law, a blatant disregard of overwhelming evidence, or a clear abuse of discretionary power will cause the court to overturn a decision of the NTSB.

Having read this far, you surely have noticed that throughout the entire process, at no point is the airman entitled to a jury trial. This is because an FAA enforcement action is an administrative matter rather than a civil or criminal situation.

When and if it finally gets to a law court, it is at the appeal level, which does not allow for a jury. A jury is a trier of **facts** and in FAA enforcement cases, the facts are determined by the ALJ way back in the early stages of the process.

# Chapter 6

# Authority of the NTSB

## It is NOT Criminal - Therefore there are NO Constitutional Protections in FAA Enforcement Actions

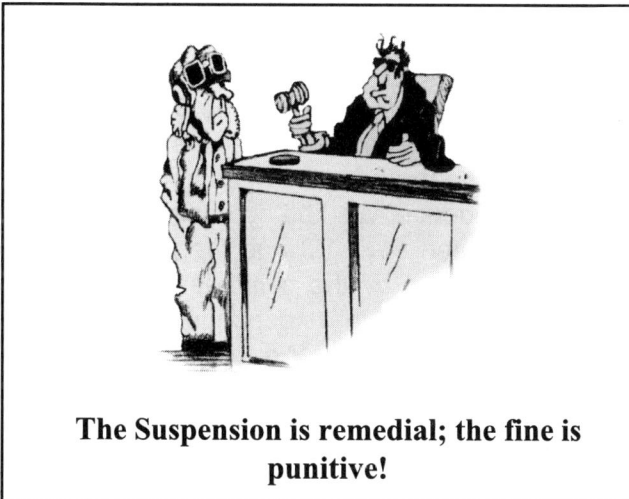

**The Suspension is remedial; the fine is punitive!**

Airpersons charged with violations of the Federal Air Regulations have consistently attempted to claim various constitutional protections, specifically the Fifth Amendment protection against self-incrimination and the Fourth Amendment protection guaranteeing due process. The courts, just as consistently, turned them down. The claim is that FAA enforcement actions are administrative in nature, and that an airman certificate is a privilege and not a license.

With certain well-defined exceptions, hearsay evidence is excluded and not admissible in our law courts, but this is not the case in enforcement actions against airpeople. In a 1992 case (*Administrator v. Hodges*, NTSB Order No. EA-3546, April 16,1992), the respondent, Hodges, had his certificate suspended for an alleged unauthorized entry into the New York Terminal Control Area. The radar controller testified that he had tagged the target as "TCA1" and tracked it to a landing at Republic Airport. The controller then called that still-unidentified target as traffic for a commuter airplane, whose pilot identified it as a Piper Seneca. Next, the controller called Republic Tower, which confirmed that the landing Seneca belonged to Hodges. The controller forwarded a certified copy of the airport's landing records to the Flight Standards District Office. The FAA attorney also introduced the ARTS radar tracking record showing the route taken by TCA1 from the time it was tagged until it was on short final at Republic Airport.

On appeal Hodges, through his attorney, argued that both the computerized tracking data and the report of a sighting by an unidentified commuter pilot should have been excluded as hearsay as they would be in a regular law court. The Board turned down this argument, saying: "Hearsay evidence is admissible in administrative proceedings, with its hearsay quality bearing only on the weight to be accorded such evidence. We find no basis to reject evidence of communications between the ATC and the pilot of the commuter aircraft, routinely recorded by the controller contemporaneous to the event. We find further that respondent's challenge to the computer data is without merit. We reject the suggestion that whenever such data is used the Administrator must affirmatively prove its accuracy. Instead, as the Administrator notes, the accuracy of the ARTS data may be assumed, *in this case at least.* (emphasis added) The ARTS system is critical to the operations of the New York's Group 1 TCA, and the equipment is tested to ensure it is operating within acceptable norms. Respondent suggests no reason to believe it was not working properly on April 30, 1987 and we see no basis to conclude it was not."

More recently, the Board went even further. Until *Administrator v. Repacholi,* NTSB Order No. EA-3888, May 26, 1993, the Board had always held double hearsay, or hearsay within hearsay, to be inadmissible, but with that case the rules changed once again in favor of the FAA. The decision says, "We regard the proper approach to hearsay within hearsay as nearly identical to that applicable to hearsay itself. The law judge may weigh it, taking into account its remoteness and reliability. Where hearsay within hearsay carries with it sufficient indicia of trustworthiness and the interests of justice will best be served by admission of the statement into evidence, we do not see why it should be deemed inadmissible or insufficient to provide a substantive basis for a decision....'(The exhibit) was considered, not by jurors with little or no experience in the weighing of evidence, but by an administrative law judge experienced in discriminating between the credible and incredible, between trustworthy and untrustworthy evidence."

Can you imagine a law court admitting the testimony of witnesses by telephone where the demeanor of witnesses is one of the factors to be taken into consideration by the trier of fact (judge or jury) in determining the credibility of the witnesses? I can't. Cross-examination by speakerphone? That's just what happened in the case of *Administrator v. Peretti*, NTSB Order No. EA-3647, August 11, 1992.

In this case, Peretti, Pilot in Command of a United Parcel Service flight was charged with violation of FAR 91.75(b) and of course 91.9 (now 91.13 - careless and reckless). While taxiing he had failed to hold short of a specified runway.

Also aboard the aircraft were two other crewmembers, a First Officer and a Flight Engineer. The First Officer received and acknowledged the ground controller's hold-short instruction. Peretti testified that he had asked both other crewmembers if he was cleared to cross the runway as he taxied and both had responded "Yes."

The First Officer testified over the telephone contrary to what the pilot had said, and this testimony was taken over respondent's lawyer's bitter objection. The reason this kind of testimony was admitted was the fact that the First Officer was in an advanced state of pregnancy at the time of the hearing. The Flight Engineer was sworn by a court reporter that was present and identified the witness. The testimony of the First Officer was that she did not tell Peretti that he was cleared to cross the runway. She also testified that she never heard Peretti ask if they were "cleared to cross" -- nor did she hear anyone tell him he was cleared to cross the runway. Respondent's attorney cross-examined the witness (over the telephone) and the law judge found against respondent.

On appeal to the full Board, the admission of the telephone testimony by the law judge was approved. In its decision the Board says: "Respondent's claim that he was denied the right to confront the 'sole eyewitness' presented in the Administrator's case-in-chief is based on legal principles inapplicable here. He relies on cases citing the Confrontation Clause of the US Constitution (Amendment VI) and which, as the Administrator points out in his reply brief involve criminal prosecutions, not civil or administrative hearings.

The only non-criminal case cited by respondent in his assertions, *Greene v. McElroy*, 360 U.S. 474 (1959), is also inopposite. In that case an individual's loss of his security clearance and job was based on anonymous allegations against which he was unable to defend effectively. Here, notwithstanding respondent's exaggerated characterization of the Flight Engineer as the 'sole eyewitness' presented by the Administrator in his case-in-chief, he knew the identity of the Flight Engineer and the First Officer, who testified in rebuttal, and he had the opportunity to cross-examine both of them, albeit by telephone in one instance. Respondent fails to articulate any actual prejudice which was caused to him by the use of telephonic testimony in these proceedings. Since the witness was sworn and subject to cross-examination, there is no basis to find that respondent was denied a fair hearing."

Note that in this case the lack of opportunity to observe the demeanor of the witness was never brought up by Peretti's counsel and thus not addressed by the Board.

In yet another case, the Board reaffirmed its position that enforcement actions are not criminal in nature and therefore do not afford the accused violator the constitutional protections of a criminal defendant. In *Administrator v. Jones,* NTSB Order No. EA-3876, April 29, 1993, Jones, believing he was under criminal investigation, refused to present his logbook for inspection by the FAA pursuant to FAR 61.51(d). He claimed the privilege of immunity from self-incrimination under the Fifth Amendment of the Constitution, whereupon the FAA revoked his private pilot certificate until such time as he might comply with the request to produce the logbook.

He appealed the revocation to the Board, which held that the Fifth Amendment does not apply in administrative cases, citing *Administrator v. Weinstein,* NTSB Order No. EA-3675 (1992), in which the Board held that the Administrator has the absolute right to review respondent's logbook so long as the request is reasonable (whatever **that** might be).

The US Circuit Court of Appeals in *US v. Manapat*, 928 F. 2d 1097 (11 Cir. 1991), found the FAA Medical Application Form to be misleading, confusing, ambiguous, and fundamentally unfair. Because she checked "NO" to the two questions on the FAA Medical Application form asking for "Record of traffic convictions" and "Record of other convictions", when in fact she did indeed have a record of such convictions, she was criminally charged with "knowingly and willfully" making false statements to the FAA. A US District Court Judge dismissed the indictment because, to him, as they appear on the form the two questions are "vague, misleading, confusing, ambiguous, and so fundamentally unfair that it amounts to a denial of due process."

The Eleventh Circuit US Circuit Court of Appeals affirmed the dismissal, accepting Manapat's argument that the application form is so confusing that it invites one to inadvertently check the wrong answer without realizing the implications of doing so. In its opinion, the court said the following: "The application form, which was fIlled out at the doctor's office, included a 'Medical History'. Within this medical history the form asked for twenty-four 'Conditions'. The first twenty-one of the 'conditions' were medical in nature. Questions twenty-two and twenty-three asked about convictions. The twenty-fourth was again medical in nature. We cannot accept the government's argument that a reasonable applicant would not be confused by this configuration of questions. It is conceivable that an applicant might believe that the form was asking for convictions that might somehow be related to medical conditions. Or an applicant could fail to understand the importance of such questions on a form concerning medical conditions and simply not give proper thought before answering. Or, more likely, an applicant in generally good health could routinely check off the many items on the standardized form without reading them carefully, resulting in an inaccurate response. Although the single statements 'Record of traffic convictions' or 'Record of other convictions' may not be ambiguous standing alone, they become quite confusing when buried in a list headed 'Medical History' and purportedly concerned with medical conditions".

The Manapat case caused the FAA to change the Medical Application form, but even before the revised form came out, the Board refused to follow Manapat in every case, stating that each case must be judged on its own merits. This principle was propounded in *Administrator v. Barghelame*, NTSB Order No. EA-3430, November 5, 1991. Here the Board said that the Court's holding in *Manapat* is not controlling in "falsification" cases over which the Board has review authority. The Board said, "With all due respect to the majority decision in *Manapat*, we do not agree that the two questions on the form concerning convictions are confusing in any respect that would likely cause a person of ordinary intelligence to entertain any genuine doubt as to their meaning. To be sure, an applicant may well find it puzzling that an application presumably seeking only medical information would be asking about matters that, at least superficially, or to a layman, do not appear to be medical in nature. An applicant may also question the placement of such questions on a medical certificate application under the heading of 'Medical History - Conditions'. However, even if we believed that an applicant's ability to honestly answer questions on the form may be undermined by a lack of understanding or knowledge of the utility of the information requested on the application, an applicant who assesses the relevance of questions on convictions is not likely to have been misled or confused. In any event, as to those individuals who, for whatever reason, answer the questions on convictions inaccurately, we see no reason not to rely on our law judges to determine whether the false responses were deliberate or were intended to deceive."

For a final look at the difference between law courts and administrative tribunals, we can consider the case of *Administrator v. Derrow* NTSB Order No. EA3590, May 29, 1992. In a routine plea bargain, the government is bound to honor whatever deal the prosecuting attorney and the defendant enter into that is approved by the judge. In the Derrow case, a "Memorandum of Understanding" was agreed to, under which Derrow pled guilty to criminal racketeering (18 US C. Sec. 1952) as a result of his involvement as a pilot for a drug trafficking enterprise. The Memorandum of Understanding provided, among other things, that the US Attorney "will seek no further prosecutions" for any acts relating to the criminal charge.

The FAA then revoked Derrow's commercial pilot certificate and his flight instructor certificate, from which revocation he appealed, claiming that he did not know his airman certificates would be affected by his plea of guilty. His appeal was denied, the Board holding that an FAA proceeding to revoke his airman certificates was not a further prosecution by the US Attorney and therefore did not contravene the Memorandum of Understanding.

### Sanctions - Their Appropriateness and the Ability of Administrative Law Judges to Modify Them

From time to time the FAA publishes a list of guidelines as to the penalties it expects to extract from regulation violators. It is assumed that the ALJs will apply the proposed sanctions as per the list. However, it doesn't always work that way, and when an ALJ modifies the sanction sought by the Friendly Feds, the FAA often appeals to the full NTSB, asking the Board to reinstate the FAA proposed sanction (or even to increase it).

Back in 1975, in the case of *Administrator v. Muzquiz* the Muzquiz doctrine was established as the rule guiding ALJs in the imposition of sanctions. This doctrine holds that administrative law judges may not modify (reduce) sanctions imposed by the FAA if the agency proves all its allegations without offering clear and compelling reasons. However, the more recent Civil Penalty Assessment Act says that the NTSB is bound by "written agency (meaning FAA) policy guidelines available to the public relating to sanctions to be imposed under this subsection unless the Board finds that any such interpretation is arbitrary, capricious, or otherwise not in accordance with the law." This would seem to put a limit on "clear and compelling reasons" and limit the judges' ability to take mitigating circumstances into account. The case I mentioned in Chapter 1, where the ALJ knocked down a mandatory sixty-day suspension of a pilot certificate to what amounted to no penalty at all (ten days in the past during which the pilot hadn't flown at all), provides a good example of a "clear and compelling reason".

In 1991, the Board was quite willing to reverse a law judge's reduction of sanction and reinstate the FAA penalty as evidenced by the case of *Administrator v. McKinley*, NTSB Order No. EA-3275, March 25, 1991. In this case, the FAA issued an emergency order of revocation of McKinley's pilot certificate claiming that he had violated FAR 91.123 and 91.13 for repeatedly refusing to turn right to avoid a possible traffic conflict as instructed by ATC. (He had requested a left turn to put him on course, and his request had been denied.) On appeal to the ALJ, the respondent contended that the traffic was nine miles away, well below him, and thus did not create a traffic conflict. The ALJ found for the Administrator, but reduced the sanction to a 180-day suspension on the basis of the fact that the conduct did not indicate a lack of qualification. The FAA appealed to the full Board, which reinstated the revocation, stating that, "Respondent's contumacious and repeated refusals to comply with ATC's instructions that he turn right to avoid traffic reflected contempt for ATC's authority to exercise control over his aircraft and a dangerous willingness both to substitute his judgment for ATC's in matters affecting air traffic management safety and to ignore ATC's instructions with which he disagreed. An airman displaying such a negative compliance disposition lacks the care, judgment and responsibility required of a certificate holder because the likelihood of his adherence of regulatory requirements adopted to promote air safety cannot be predicted with any degree of confidence. Revocation is, therefore, the appropriate sanction for the violations the law judge sustained."

And in 1992, *Muzquiz* was strictly applied by the Board. In *Administrator v. Marrone*, NTSB Order No. EA-3661, August 13, 1992, the Board held that even though all the "charges" (the language used in *Muzquiz*) were not proven, a law judge may not reduce the sanction if the Administrator proves all the "violations" alleged, unless the ALJ offers "clear and compelling" reasons for doing so. In this case, Marrone had his inspection authorization revoked by the FAA for signing off a shoddy inspection done by another, an "inspection" that left the airplane with several uncorrected discrepancies. The law judge reduced the sanction to an eight-month suspension and the FAA appealed. On appeal, Morrone's attorney cited *Administrator v. Pearson*, 3 NTSB 3837 (1981), claiming that *Muzquiz* only applied when the FAA has proven all of the "charges", which means all of the factual allegations in the Administrator's complaint. The violation was proven, but not all of the factual allegations, and the law judge therefore reduced the sanction. The full Board reinstated the revocation, saying, "Although *Pearson* used the word 'charges' in place of *Muzquiz*'s 'violations', our intent has been clear and did not change. We intended to apply and have applied the *Muzquiz* standard when the Administrator has proven that respondent violated the cited regulations. Thus, use of the word 'charges' in place of 'violations' produced no change in meaning."

Now compare these 1991 and 1992 cases with the 1994 one that follows, in which the Board, citing ample reasons, gave its law judges a great deal more power to modify the sanctions sought by the agency.

The NTSB threw out the Murquiz doctrine in *Hinson v. Glassburn* (NTSB Docket SW 12919, July 5, 1994) when it said, "The law judge will have had the opportunity to make his judgment after observation of the Administrator's case and first hand evaluation of the evidence and witness demeanor. These are factors that are traditionally understood to warrant the allowance of some deference by reviewing authorities to the discretionary choices of hearing officers." In the Glassburn case, the ALJ had knocked down the FAA's 120-day suspension of Glassburns' mechanic certificate to 30 days. The FAA appealed, claiming that the administrative law judge had failed to state "clear and compelling" reasons for the reduction as required by the *Murquiz* doctrine. The Board, using the above language, dismissed the appeal. The following cases shed some light on just how the Board views ALJs modifying FAA sanctions. Compare those decided by the Board prior to 1994 with those decided after that date.

Prior to the change in the attitude of the Board toward permitting the law judges to impose their own judgment, they continued to reverse its judges for reducing penalties based on mitigating circumstances. In the case of *Administrator v. Pringel*, NTSB Order No. EA-3265, March 5, 1991, the Board reinstated a 120-day suspension that the law judge had knocked down to 45 days. He took this action because Pringel was under great emotional and financial stress, had a violation-free record, and used his certificate to earn his living. The full Board, in reinstating the 120-day suspension, said, "The Board has repeatedly rejected adverse economic consequences or a violation-free record as justification for decreasing sanction. We do not think that any emotional of financial stress that respondent faced should justify a reduction in sanction. It may be expedient or financially advantageous for a person not to comply with the comprehensive program the Administrator has devised to ensure air safety. However, compromising safety to further a personal interest adverse to safety does not deserve consideration as a mitigating factor for purpose of calculating sanction."

But even after the apparent change in the attitude of the Board, there are some things for which they will not allow the ALJs to reduce the sanction of the FAA. In the case of *Administrator v. Nave*, NTSB Order No. EA-4257, September 27, 1994, the ALJ reduced the FAA sanction from emergency revocation of Nave's private pilot certificate for drug convictions and the subsequent falsification of two medical applications to an eight-month suspension on the basis of the respondent had rehabilitated himself. The Board reinstated the revocation, stating that **any** conviction involving the sale of drugs warrants airman certificate revocation.

In 1995, the Board determined that an ALJ dismissal of part of the Administrator's complaint does not warrant an automatic reduction in the sanction sought. In the case of *Administrator v. Ribar*, NTSB Order No. 4318, January 19,1995, the FAA charged Ribar with low level flying over a congested area and an abnormally steep take-off. The law judge found for the FAA as to the low flying, but dismissed the steep take-off charge. He therefore reduced the FAA imposed penalty of a 60-day suspension of respondent's commercial pilot certificate to a 30-day suspension. The agency appealed and the full Board reinstated the 60-day suspension, holding that, "While dismissal of one or more allegations from a complaint is a circumstance that may well result in a finding that a lower sanction than that originally sought by the Administrator should be affirmed, it does not justify an automatic or formula reduction in the sanction in all cases. Rather the law judge in such instances must evaluate the seriousness of the charges he has found proved and form his judgment on sanction by reference to precedent and such other sources as may be helpful or necessary in the interest of furthering uniformity." A 60-day certificate suspension is consistent with Board precedent, so they reinstated the FAA penalty.

Before leaving the subject of the authority of the ALJs and the Board itself, it is appropriate to consider two other cases that limit that authority.

In the first of these, *Administrator v. Nixon,* NTSB Order No. EA-4249, September 8, 1994, the Board asserted that it had no authority to change the nature of a sanction. Nixon had appealed a 30-day certificate suspension for low flying, requesting remedial training instead. In denying Nixon's appeal, the Board held that, "We have no authority to substitute an administrative action (such as a warning notice, letter of correction, or a remedial training program) for a legal enforcement action (such as certificate action or a civil penalty)."

Finally, if the Board believes that it cannot change the nature of an agency sanction, they will certainly not permit their law judges to do so. This is illustrated by the case of *Administrator v. Hemphill,* NTSB Order No-EA-3703, October 20, 1992. In this instance, Hemphill was found to have violated FAR 91.88 by entering an ARSA without having established two-way communications with ATC and FAR 91.9 for being careless in doing so. The agency imposed a 30-day suspension of his pilot certificate, and the law judge reduced it to 15 days, conditional upon Hemphill visiting an Air Traffic Control facility and submitting a written report to the law judge relating what he learned during this visit. The FAA appealed and the full Board reversed the law judge and reinstated the 30-day suspension, stating, "It was improper for the law judge to assess an additional penalty wholly independent from the sanction sought by the Administrator."

PART 5
PROTECTION AND DEFENSE

## Chapter 7

# Aviation Safety Reporting System Cases and The Airman's Authority to Deviate from Regulatory Procedures in an Emergency Situation

Back in Chapters 1 and 5, we discussed the NASA Aviation Safety Reporting System, how it may provide immunity from sanction in enforcement actions, and the limitations therein. Now, let us look at how the FAA legal system handles these matters. As pointed out, one of the limitations to the airman's ability to claim immunity from sanction after the timely filing of an ASRS report is that it must be inadvertent rather than deliberate. It is in this area that most of the controversy has arisen.

In the case of *Administrator v. Copsey*, NTSB Order No. EA-3448, November 25, 1991, respondent Copsey was charged with flying an unairworthy aircraft. This case is also particularly interesting because it demonstrates the NTSB's proclivity to place more credence on the testimony of the FAA witness than on that of the airman in terms of what each defines as "airworthy". The facts are as follows: While parking an aircraft, Cropsey had a prop strike. The left prop of the Cessna 402 struck a cable. On examining the prop, respondent Cropsey determined it to be airworthy and proceeded to fly it to his destination where he was met by two FAA inspectors who examined the prop and determined it to be "unairworthy".

Respondent Cropsey filed a timely ASRS report and at the ALJ hearing claimed immunity from sanction. The law judge granted him immunity and the Administrator appealed to the full board, which reversed the ALJ and ruled in favor of the FAA, stating, "In our view, the substantial evidence of record supports a finding that respondent knew the propeller was unairworthy but chose to fly to Albuquerque anyway, thereby demonstrating conduct that was deliberate and not inadvertent. In short, his decision to take off in an unairworthy aircraft in violation of the applicable FAR, and without obtaining a ferry permit, renders him ineligible for a waiver of sanction under the ASRP as that program has been administered under Advisory Circular 00-46C."

However, by 1996, the Board was beginning to accept as credible the testimony of airmen as demonstrated by its ruling in the case of *Administrator v. Ferguson*, NTSB No. EA-4457, May 15, 1996. Here, again, the Board was differentiating between "deliberate" and "inadvertent" and here again, the Board's decision was based in large measure on the credibility of the airman's testimony. In this case, respondent Ferguson was charged with operating his aircraft with ice and icicles on the elevator control system in violation of FAR 135.227(a) and 91.13(a), and the FAA ordered a 45-day suspension of his pilot certificate. By the bye, have you noticed that in the vast majority of cases the FAA throws in 91.13 (formerly 91.9) "Careless and Reckless"? This is done on the theory that almost any violation is the result of a careless and reckless act or omission, but for careless and reckless to apply, the act must demonstrate a "wanton disregard for the safety of others."

Ferguson had timely filed a "NASA Report" and claimed immunity from sanction under the provisions of the Aviation Safety Reporting Program. The FAA refused to waive the 45-day suspension on the ground that the violation was not inadvertent, but rather it was deliberate. Ferguson appealed and the NTSB ALJ sustained the violation, but waived the sanction because of the timely filing of the report. The law judge believed the pilot's testimony that he had inspected the elevator surface and found no ice, and that the ice had formed after his inspection, from an ice pellet shower that arose after the preflight inspection and just prior to take-off. Both sides appealed to the full Board, and the Board denied both appeals, permitting the law judge's decision to stand. The Board, in supporting the decision of the ALJ, found that the pilot's action in this matter had not been wanton or gross, and in fact had been inadvertent. In reaching its decision the Board cited the cases of *Administrator v. Fay, 7 NTSB 051 (1991)* and *Ferguson v. NTSB*, 678 F.2d 821 (9th Cir. 1982).

In the case of *Administrator v. Schuttler*, NTSB Order No. EA-

3487, January 27, 1992, the Board, again determined the difference between acts that are deliberate and those which are inadvertent. Placing their focus on this principle, the Board refused to waive the sanction of suspending respondent Schuttler's ATP certificate for violating FAR 121.548, refusing an FAA inspector "free and uninterrupted access to the forward observer's jumpseat of the flight deck of the airliner commanded by Schuttler". The airman had filed a timely report under the Aviation Safety Reporting Program and he claimed a waiver of sanction. The ALJ found for the Administrator as to the violation, but granted Schuttler his request for the waiver of the penalty of suspension. The FAA appealed, and the Board reversed the law judge, saying, "Turning to the Administrator's appeal, the law judge focused in the initial decision on whether respondent's actions were 'inadvertent and not deliberate' so as to come within the terms of the ASRP. We agree with the Administrator that this analysis is inconsistent with our decision in *Administrator v. Crim*, 3 NTSB 2471 (1980), where we held that the denial of access to the cockpit is conduct which does not fall within the parameters of the ASRP."

On the whole, it seems that the Board has been quite generous in liberally allowing waivers of sanction to airpeople who file NASA reports. In the case of *Administrator v. Halbert*, NTSB Order No. EA-3628, July 10,1992, respondent Halbert was found to be in violation of FAR 91.29 and 91.9 (now 91.13) by continuing to fly a multi-engine aircraft beyond a suitable landing airport after the precautionary shut down of one of its engines, contrary to regulations, and he claimed a waiver of sanction under the terms of the Aviation Safety Reporting Program. One of the conditions required for the granting of such waiver is that the report be mailed within ten days of the event. The person filing the report "must prove that within 10 days after the violation, he or she completed and delivered or mailed a written report of the incident or occurrence to NASA". The proof offered by Halbert was a NASA strip date stamped 11 days after the incident. In other words, NASA received it 11 days after the event. Any normal person would know that to be received on the 11th day it would of necessity have to have been mailed at the very latest one day prior to that and thus within the 10-day window.

However, in its infinite stupidity, the FAA appealed the law judge's granting of the waiver of penalty. They cited FAA Advisory

Circular, AC No. 00-46C, which describes the Aviation Safety Reporting Program, including the fact that a report, in order to support a claim of immunity from sanction must be **sent** within 10 days of the violation. The Administrator's ridiculous argument was that respondent Halbert did not timely file the report with NASA and is thus precluded from a waiver of sanction under the program. In turning down this foolish argument the Board said, "It can be assumed that a report received by NASA eleven days after the incident was mailed within ten days of the incident."

## The Airman's Emergency Authority

Entirely different from the waiver of sanction granted by the Aviation Safety Reporting Program in which the violation stands on the record and only the penalty is forgiven, the authority of an airman to deviate from regulatory procedures in cases where an emergency exists is absolute, and all violations are forgiven. However, as is usually the case, there are certain restrictions on the conditions under which an airperson may be forgiven a deviation after having declared an emergency. In essence, the airman must do all in his power to avoid the emergency, and it most certainly must not have been of his own making.

Every airperson is aware that he or she may take whatever action is necessary in response to an emergency situation, but most of them are very reluctant to declare the existence of an emergency situation for fear of the ensuing investigation or at the very least an aversion to the imagined volume of paperwork and reports required to justify the declaration of an emergency. What many pilots fail to realize is that it is not necessary to verbally declare an emergency before exercising the emergency power to deviate from the regulations, although it certainly makes it easier to justify such action.

As usual, the NTSB, leaving the interpretation of its own regulations to the FAA, provides us with insight as to just how they can be expected to interpret their orders and rulings. The cases that follow serve to demonstrate just how the Board views this emergency authority.

According to FAR 91.3, 'in an in-flight emergency requiring immediate action, the pilot-in-command may deviate from any rule of CFR 14, Part 91, General Operating and Flight Rules to the extent required to meet that emergency." The case of *Administrator v. Worth*, NTSB Order No. EA-3595, June 2, 1992, serves to demonstrate the fact that the Board expects airmen to act responsibly and use good judgment notwithstanding their ability to deviate from the rules in the face of an emergency. Respondent Worth wanted to make a short VFR flight of some 95 nautical miles. He received no less than three weather briefings from Flight Service, delaying his departure after each of the first two because the weather was below VFR minimums, but improving.

By the time he received the third briefing, the weather had improved to marginal VFR and was forecast to continue to improve, so he took off. You guessed it. Instead of improving, the weather deteriorated. Approximately 20 miles short of his destination, the ceiling and visibility had lowered to below VFR minimums. He found himself in a snow shower and his airplane began to ice up. A turn back from whence he had come was not an option since the weather had deteriorated behind him. His attempts to use the radio were marginal at best due to an intermittent short in his antenna. Fortunately, he finally effected a safe landing at Spokane, after hearing a faint clearance to land. His original destination was some 20 miles from Spokane. The FAA busted him and charged him with operating VFR in weather below minimum VFR conditions, with operating within the Spokane ARSA without first having established radio contact with ATC as required, and with being careless.

Respondent Worth defended himself by claiming that he was exercising his emergency authority when he deviated from the regulations. When the case reached the NTSB on appeal, the Board found the first violation to be excused on the ground that Worth had indeed legitimately exercised his emergency authority. However, they found that the emergency authority did not excuse the second violation. They also found him to have been careless, and ordered a 45-day suspension of his private pilot certificate. In reaching its decision, the Board opined that when one takes off into marginal VFR he is taking a calculated risk that the weather might worsen, even in the face of a forecast for improvement.

If it does worsen, they said, the predicament in which the airman finds himself is of his own making as opposed to conditions that would not have been reasonably anticipated. Thus, the violation is not excusable as a weather emergency. They further found the penetration of the

ARSA without communication with ATC to have been excusable because the radio problems were unexpected and not of his own making. Finally, they found him to indeed be careless for failing to squawk the appropriate codes on his transponder, once he was aware of his radio difficulties.

In determining the reasonableness of an airman's actions when the emergency defense is asserted, rather than apply the "reasonable man" rule of the law courts, the Board will defer to the Administrator in the FAA's interpretation of its own rules. This is exemplified by the decision on the case of *Administrator v. Russo*, NTSB Order No. EA-3800, February 10, 1993. This case also serves to illustrate the limits the Board will place on granting waivers of sanction in those instances in which a timely ASRS report has been filed with NASA.

Respondent Russo had his ATP certificate suspended for 60 days for operating an aircraft carelessly in violation of FAR 91.9 (now 91.13 - Careless and Reckless). Russo advised ATC that he was fuel critical, using the language, "we have minimum fuel" in response to ATC's query as to whether he wished to declare an emergency. He declined to formally declare an emergency.

Respondent Russo was advised that Republic Airport (his intended destination) was closed because of inoperative runway lights, but that the closer Islip airport was available. However, Russo opted to proceed to Republic, where he landed safely after making an abrupt right turn followed immediately by an abrupt left turn at a very low altitude to get lined up with the runway, according to the testimony of the controller.

When respondent Russo appealed the FAA's suspension order, the ALJ ruled in favor of the Administrator. From this ruling, Russo appealed to the full Board, which also ruled for the Administrator, stating: "The record overwhelmingly supports the fact that respondent knew the difference between declaring an emergency and stating that he had a minimum fuel situation. He chose the latter. Even when pressed by ATC, he refused to declare an emergency, and as the law judge pointed out in his decision, when the warning light actually indicated that an emergency situation might soon exist, respondent, who was still in contact with ATC, failed even then to declare an emergency. In the Board's view, if an emergency existed, it did not occur until after respondent chose to bypass Islip Airport. He knew that Republic Airport was closed when he had ample time and opportunity to execute a safe landing at Islip Airport. His decision to bypass Islip and land at Republic Airport, when Republic Airport was closed, evidenced clearly deficient judgment, and supports the finding of a violation of FAR Section 91.9."

The Board also refused to waive the suspension of respondent Russo's ATP certificate even though a timely report was filed under the Aviation Safety Reporting Program because, "In the Board's view, the fact that respondent chose to bypass Islip and land at Republic makes his careless act deliberate and not inadvertent, taking it outside the parameters of the ASRP."

The NTSB does allow airmen some leeway in the exercise of their emergency authority, as evidenced by the case of *Administrator v. Scott*, NTSB Order No. EA-4003, October 15, 1993. In this case, respondent Scott made a choice between landing his transport category airplane (loaded beyond the maximum allowable landing weight) and remaining in the air for an additional 30 minutes while fuel was dumped to get the aircraft below the maximum landing weight. Scott had been advised by his company dispatch to return to his departure airport and land because of a potential maintenance problem. This message had been relayed through ATC. Scott, therefore, didn't know the nature of the potential problem, and since the airplane was only slightly over the maximum landing weight, he made the decision to land rather than delay the landing for the half-hour required for the fuel dumping process.

As it turned out, there was no maintenance problem at all and the flight could have proceeded to its destination rather than having to return to the departure airport. The dear old FAA issued an order suspending Scott's ATP certificate for 60 days for landing the aircraft overweight in violation of FAR 91.31(c) - Compliance with Operating Limitations, and (look out, here it comes again) 91.9 (now 91.13), Careless or Reckless.

The ALJ found that the violation had indeed been committed, but he reduced the sanction to a 15-day suspension. On appeal to the full board, the Board reversed the finding of violation, asserting that Scott had properly exercised his emergency authority, stating, ".....performed a thorough analysis of the implications of an overweight landing vis-a-vis fuel dumping. Respondent testified, unrebutted, that this was extremely light, as overweight landings go, and he established that conditions for the landing were excellent and met those prescribed in the flight manual by wide margins. Respondent felt that, not knowing exactly what was wrong, an overweight landing was necessary, as dumping fuel would add 30 minutes to the flight."

## Chapter 8

## The FAA's Much-Abused Power of Emergency Revocation

As we discussed way back in Chapter 1, the Administrator, quite rightly, has the power to instantly revoke an airperson's certificate if, but only if, there would exist a continuing imminent threat to public safety if the airperson were to be permitted to retain his or her privileges during the pendency of an enforcement action. The problem has been that the agency, flouting the rulings of the NISB, has continued to invoke its right to take immediate action to revoke a certificate when there has been no danger to the public whatever. It is, however, in this area that we see a glimmer of hope that perhaps the FAA is being forced into at least a bit of accountability.

The landmark case in this area, the one that has guided the NTSB in all its subsequent decisions, is the *Frank* case (*Daryl R. Frank et al v. James B. Busey, FAA Administrator*, Case No. 91-1469).

Writing in the Summer 1993 issue of the **LPBA Journal** (the journal of the Lawyer Pilots Bar Association), Vincent A. Butler had this to say about the *Frank* case: "In October of 1991, the US Court of Appeals for the District of Columbia Circuit took the first move towards harnessing the increasing abuse of the statutory authority utilized by the Federal Aviation Administration with regards to the issuance of Emergency Orders of Revocation."

Back in 1972, in *United States v. Harper,* 335 F. Supp 904, the Court had said that a Section 609 Emergency Order "might be regarded as analogous to a judicial temporary restraining order issued *ex parte* in an emergency." In 1980, in *Nevada Airlines v. Bond*, F 2d 1017, the 9th Circuit declared that the Court has jurisdiction to exercise oversight review of these discretionary decisions of the Administrator. This set the stage for *Frank*, the facts of which case gave the court ample opportunity to curb the discretionary power of the Administrator.

The Detroit Flight Standards District Office (FSDO) had been investigating Active Aero Charters, Inc. of Ypsilanti, Michigan for some 12 months by September 4, 1991. On that day, the office of the FAA Great Lakes Regional Counsel issued Emergency Orders of Revocation against seven of Active Aero's line pilots, alleging violation of flight and duty time, which violations were alleged to have occurred 18 months previously.

This is an emergency situation? To revoke their certificates now, 18 months after the violation occurred? Where's the emergency? The imminent threat to safety? Obviously (to any reasonable human being), there was no such threat. For those of us who operate in the jurisdiction of the Detroit FSDO, this sort of activity is not surprising in the least. Only in the Detroit FSDO would they be foolish enough to claim this situation constituted an emergency. The Court decided that this blatant abuse of power had gone on long enough and called a screeching halt to it, and *Frank* provided the perfect vehicle for the court to act.

In his review of the case in the **LPBA Journal**, Butler goes on to say: "In *Daryl R. Frank, et al*, the Court gave the Office of the FAA Chief Counsel.... every opportunity to submit such facts and/or reasons that would justify the use of its emergency authority under these circumstances, a 'last resort' remedy, but the Administrator was unable to satisfy the Court in any fashion. Therefore, the FAA agreed to withdraw the 'emergency' aspect of its Order(s) of Revocation so that each Pilot could continue to earn a livelihood while these consolidated cases were litigated before the Office of the NTSB Administrative Law Judges.

"....a Petition for Extraordinary Writ, or in the Alternative, Petition for Review was filed concurrently with the... Motion for Stay. As a result of the pendency of that Petition (asking the Court to review the constitutionality of the Emergency Revocation Authority from a due process standpoint) and the very favorable decision(s) entered by NTSB Administrative Law Judge William R. Mullins, the Administrator not only agreed to a very favorable settlement with regards to said Pilots and their employer/air carrier, Active Air Charters, Inc. but also agreed to reimburse the Respondents the sum of $15,000 incurred in counsel fees without the necessity of an EAJA Application."

One would suppose that since that glorious day when the *Frank* decision was rendered, the agency would have commenced to exercise a modicum of restraint with respect to the exercise of its emergency revocation power, but such has not been the case. Every single one of these so-called emergencies has to be tried individually, and in a great many of them the FAA continues to lose. In case the message hasn't been clear enough, the important thing is the fact that an emergency revocation effectively grounds the airman forthwith, while in the ordinary prosecution of a violation case the airperson is permitted to continue to exercise the privileges of his or her certificate until the matter is finally adjudicated by an ALJ, the NTSB, or the Court.

Prior to *Frank*, the Board had refused to limit the Administrator's use of the emergency revocation technique as evidenced by a couple of 1990 cases. In the first of these, *Administrator v. Sallee's Aviation, Inc.*, NTSB Order No. EA-3185, August 28, 1990, the respondent, by virtue of having its Operating Certificate revoked under the emergency power, was effectively put out of business during the pendency of the hearing. He complained, contending that some other action of the Administrator would be more appropriate and would permit him to continue to earn a livelihood while the enforcement action was ongoing. In sustaining the Administrator and affirming the emergency nature of the revocation, the Board said, "Respondent's.... contentions, for the most part, involve challenges to the Administrator's resort to his emergency authority in this matter and the adverse effect on respondent the selection of that enforcement track over others entails. However, inasmuch as the Board does not sit in judgment on the Administrator's exercise of his emergency powers it follows that we will not undertake to determine whether the Administrator could or should have pursued some other course of action."

One offense for which revocation has always been seen as appropriate is 'lack of qualification" to hold the grade of certificate held. This was forcibly brought home by the case of *Administrator v. Blackman*, NTSB Order No. EA-3183, 1990.

In this case, the Administrator issued an Emergency Order of Revocation of respondent Blackman's ATP certificate. They charged him with several violations, including penetrating the Detroit TCA without a clearance (the good old Detroit FSDO at work again), being in the Detroit Airport Traffic Area, without communicating with the tower, and operating faster than the allowable speed in this area. Blackman appealed to an NTSB ALJ, who found for the Administrator, and then to the full Board, which sustained the ALJ. The full Board said, in response to respondent's challenge to the appropriateness of the sanction:

"On the question of sanction, we recognize that 'minor' TCA infractions ordinarily draw no more than a sixty-day suspension. This case, however, bears scant resemblance to the more typical unauthorized TCA incursion, which frequently involves little more than a low-time pilot nicking a TCA in territory with which he is unfamiliar. Here, the respondent, an ATP certificate holder who had flown between Toledo and Detroit 'hundreds' of times, appears to have allowed himself to become so distracted from his course monitoring responsibility that he flew, while traveling at an unlawfully high speed (he was flying a Citation), directly into a TCA toward departing airline traffic. While these facts may not, in themselves, compel the judgment that respondent cannot be expected to conform his conduct to regulatory requirements, they do indicate such a conclusion when two other factors are weighed; namely, that respondent has a TCA violation history, and that respondent, once he realized he was off course and in the TCA, created an even greater potential for hazard by turning off his transponder in an apparent effort to evade detection. This latter circumstance is especially troubling, as it suggests respondent was more interested in hiding his identity from ATC than ensuring that ATC had as much information about an unauthorized, uncontrolled high speed aircraft within the TCA. Respondent is, therefore, a repeat offender who has demonstrated a willingness to compromise air safety when he believes doing so might advance his personal interests. We think such conduct by the holder of an ATP in inexcusable, and we find ourselves unable to disagree with the Administrator's judgment that respondent by his enforcement history, his violations here, and his reckless attitude toward safety has demonstrated a lack of qualifications. Thus, revocation is the appropriate sanction."

While it would be difficult to disagree with the Board's decision in *Blackman*, the emergency nature of the revocation might be questioned. Even though revocation may well be the appropriate sanction in this case, it provides another example of the free and easy use of the Administrator's emergency revocation authority.

However, by 1995 the Board was still holding airmen to very strict procedural limits. In *Administrator v. Edwards*, NTSB Order No. EA-4376, July 5, 1995, the Board reaffirmed the 1986 case of *Administrator v. Myers*, 5 NTSB 997, that, "an airman's ability to waive the applicability of the emergency rules 'does not mean that an airman's failure to comply with a time limit established by the emergency rules will be treated as a waiver of those rules or as an election to proceed under the non-emergency rules.'"

Another example of the use of the revocation sanction as an absolute is the situation in which an individual falsifies records, particularly flight time records in a logbook. In *Administrator v. Pohl*, NTSB Order No. EA-3913, June 8, 1993, the Board upheld the Administrator's emergency revocation of respondent Pohl's commercial pilot certificate for entering 131.5 hours in his logbook for a specific aircraft make and model when records of the operator for whom he worked showed only 63.9 hours.

He had offered his logbook for an FAA audit to demonstrate eligibility for the ATP certificate. On appeal the Board once again affirmed that revocation is an appropriate sanction for such an offense.

Another offense for which revocation is mandatory is a drug conviction where the defendant was found guilty of being involved "for profit or commercial purposes". In 1989, the FAA had published guidelines stating that a conviction for more than simple possession of a controlled substance (that is, for commercial gain) except in extraordinary circumstances will require certificate revocation. This applies to those convictions that involve the use of aircraft only. FAR 61.15(a)(2) mandates that a hearing must be held to determine sanction in those cases that permit either suspension or revocation, but the Board held in *Administrator v. Poole*, Order No. EA-4425, February 7, 1996 that no hearing is necessary in such cases. In this case, the FAA revoked the certificate of respondent Poole as a result of a state conviction for the sale of controlled substance. On appeal, the ALJ granted Summary Judgment in favor of the FAA's Order. Poole appealed to the full Board and the Board upheld the law judge saying, "While summary judgment is not always appropriate in Section 61.15 cases that do not involve aircraft use, it is, nevertheless, appropriate in the instant case, given respondent's conviction for more than simple possession of a controlled substance for commercial gain and the Administrator's clear policy on the effect of such a conviction on a respondent's airman certificate."

In another 1996 drug case, *Administrator v. Guslander*, NTSB Order No. EA- 4431, February 22, 1996, petitioner Guslander appealed the revocation of his private pilot certificate. The FAA Order of Revocation had been affirmed by a law judge (also by way of summary judgment), on the basis that such revocation, in addition to his criminal punishment, amounted to double jeopardy contrary to the Fifth Amendment.

In upholding the decision of the law judge, the Board said," The Board has consistently held that revocation is remedial, not punitive. It is utilized, in the interest of air safety, when an airman is deemed to lack the requisite care, judgment, and responsibility of a certificate holder."

Just as falsification of records and drug convictions mandates revocation as the appropriate sanction, so does cheating on an examination. In the case of *Administrator v. Gilley*, NTSB Report No. EA-3303, May 10, 1991, with one member dissenting, the Board affirmed the Administrator's Order of Emergency Revocation of respondent Gilley's **private pilot certificate** when he was found to have cheated on the written examination for a **mechanic certificate**. Respondent Gilley appealed the Order on the basis that the penalty was too extreme, and the law judge reduced the sanction to a six-month suspension of his private pilot certificate. Taking into account certain mitigating circumstances related to respondent's family problems, the law judge ruled that the revocation of the unrelated pilot certificate was a bit much. The Administrator appealed to the full Board, and the Board reversed the law judge and reinstated the revocation, ruling that, "Certain kinds of violations justify a conclusion that those committing them do not possess the care, judgment, and responsibility that is a prerequisite common to the holding of **any** airman certificate or rating." (emphasis added)

Although the Board and the Courts have strictly applied procedural rules, there is at least one situation where two different US Circuit Courts of Appeals have refused to do so. As repeatedly pointed out, except in an emergency situation, an FAA order suspending or revoking an airperson's certificate is stayed pending final disposition of the case by the Board (if an appeal is taken). However, if the Board is advised by the Administrator that, "an emergency exists and safety in air commerce or air transportation requires the immediate effectiveness of his order, in which case the order shall remain effective and the National Transportation Safety Board shall finally dispose of the appeal within sixty days after being so advised." This principle is codified in just that language in US C App. Section 1429(a). The purpose, of course, is to insure the affected airperson a reasonably short time in which to regain his privileges if the Board should rule that he or she is entitled to them. What this law fails to address is the effect of exceeding the 60-day time limit.

The ability of an airman to continue to exercise the privileges of his or her certificate except in cases of emergency revocation lasts through the administrative process, but if an appeal is taken to the US Circuit Court of Appeals, each case is considered separately. It is then left to the NTSB to determine whether or not the airman may keep his or her certificate pending the appeal to the Court. In *Administrator v. Ter Keurst*, NTSB Order No. EA-3656, August 11, 1992, the Board restated its position that it will consider the seriousness of the charges in determining whether or not a stay of execution of the Administrator's order will be granted pending review by the court. The Board has granted requests for a stay in cases involving a relatively short-term certificate suspension almost as a matter of routine, and has routinely denied such requests where revocation is the sanction ordered. In this case, the sanction was a 180-day suspension of respondent's pilot certificate. Because of the seriousness of the charges (low flying over an assembly of people while towing a banner and other charges), the Board said, "We agree with the Administrator that respondent's violations demonstrate a disregard for public safety that counsels against the issuance of a stay of the Board's order."

The 10th Circuit in *Gallagher v. NTSB*, F.2d refused to dismiss an FAA order of Emergency Revocation when the statutory deadline had been exceeded by two weeks. The decision was reached on jurisdictional grounds in this case. Meanwhile, the 6th Circuit, in 1992's *McCarthney v. Busey* F.2d, the airmen's certificates had been revoked by the FAA under the emergency authority. The FAA's sanctions had been reduced to various periods of suspension by the law judge, and revocations had been reinstated by the Board three days after the 60-day deadline appealed to the court. Their basis of appeal was the statutory time limit. Their claim was that the ALJ's reduction of penalty should apply since the Board had failed to act within the allotted time; this failure to take any timely action within 60 days, they said, resulted in its loss of jurisdiction to change the ALJ's decision to reduce the sanctions. Here again, the Court disagreed. It seems that the statutory time limit is not mandatory, since the statute fails to provide for a consequence for failure to comply. If this is the case, the statute is literally meaningless, and it has no effect whatever. Since that seems to be the law as set forth by the Court, what good is the statute anyway? Why have a law that has no meaning, no teeth, and no means of enforcement?

The entire matter of the Administrator's emergency revocation authority is troubling to all concerned (except the FAA). That there is a definite need for such authority in legitimate cases of a genuine threat to safety in "air commerce or air transportation" cannot be argued.

However, the blatant abuse of this power at the hands of the agency has gone a long way toward reinforcing the adversarial position that exists between the FAA and its customers, the users of the airspace.

# Chapter 9

## Section 609

## The "Stale Complaint Rule", Other Considerations of Timely Action and the Recertification Ride

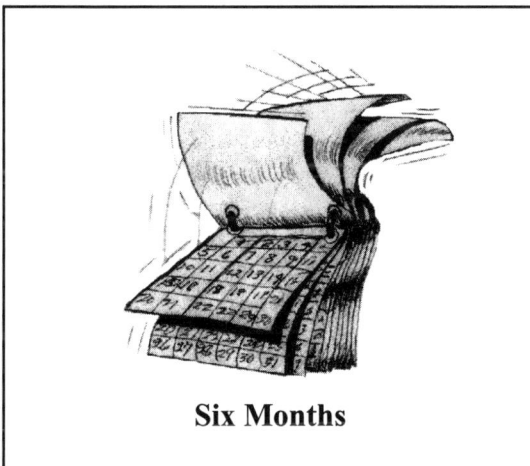

**Six Months**

# The State Complaint Rule and its Limitations

Most airmen know that after an accident, incident or minor violation they are subject to be called in for a "609 Ride" with an FAA Safety Inspector (Operations Type) to demonstrate that they still have the requisite aeronautical knowledge and skill that they demonstrated at the time they acquired the grade of certificate they hold. In fact, the issuance of a certificate implies that the "FAA giveth and the FAA can taketh away."

  This power of the agency, however, is not absolute. Certain conditions must be met before the certificate of an airman may be brought into question. There will be more on this subject later, but for now, we will consider the effect of delay, late filing, and other matters of time in relation to enforcement actions, the foremost of which is the so-called "Stale Complaint Rule," which also falls under Section 609 of the Act.

  Although the stale complaint rule is embodied in Rule 13, it is Rule 33 of the Board's rules of practice that provides for dismissal of a complaint and "states allegations of offenses that occurred more than six months prior to the Administrator's advising respondent (not the LOI, but the NOPCA) as to the reasons for proposed action under Section 609 of the Act." The specific exceptions to this rule are lack of qualification to hold the certificate (this is always cause for revocation) and in those cases where the Administrator shows good cause for delay (it is this one which is wide open to interpretation.) *Administrator v. Brea*, NTSB Order No. EA-3657, August 11, 1992 provides an excellent example of how the Board views this rule in the ordinary course of events.

  In this case, a mechanic who had completed an annual inspection of an aircraft had failed to comply with an AD (Airworthiness Directive). The Administrator first became aware of the potential violation eight months after the inspection; the Notice of Proposed Certificate Action was mailed some three months later, almost eleven months after the event. The Administrator, through his counsel, acknowledged at the hearing that the three-month delay in notifying respondent Brea was primarily because of a "typing backlog" at the regional office that was preparing the prosecution. In dismissing the Administrator's complaint as stale the Board said, "The record fails to reflect that the investigation of this matter was either sufficiently lengthy or complex in nature to fully warrant the Administrator's delay in informing respondent of the proposed certificate action.

  Moreover, the Administrator has neither asserted nor demonstrated that the processing of the case was in any way expedited so as to minimize the delay once he became aware of respondent's alleged FAR violation. Thus, we do not believe that good cause for the Administrator's delay in notifying respondent of the proposed certificate action until almost eleven months after the alleged FAR violation occurred has been established, and we, therefore, find that the complaint must be dismissed as stale under Rule 33."

Brea was affirmed over a year later when the Board ruled in *Administrator v. Holland*, NTSB Order no. EA-3387, October 12, 1993. This again upheld the law judge's dismissal of the Administrator's complaint as stale. Here, respondent Holland, a mechanic, was charged with failing to follow the manufacturer's service bulletin in performing certain maintenance as required by regulation. The notice of proposed certificate action was issued about three and one-half months after the FAA became aware of the alleged violation, and some nine months after the event. Holland moved for dismissal because his witnesses and records were no longer available since the employer for whom he worked at the time of the alleged violation was no longer in business.

The Administrator answered this motion, claiming that the FAA investigated the occurrence immediately after it was discovered. However, the answer also showed that the matter lay dormant in the legal office of the FAA's Southwest Region for over seven weeks before the Notice of Proposed Certificate Action was issued and sent to respondent Holland. The Administrator offered no reason for this delay, and the law judge dismissed his complaint. The Administrator appealed, and the Board affirmed the ALJ's dismissal, stating, "that where a violation is not discovered contemporaneously, the Administrator's belated awareness may only serve as good cause for a delay in the issuance of a NOPCA if reasonable prosecutorial diligence is exercised after the receipt of information concerning the acts which may be indicative of such a violation." In *Holland*, the Board quoted its *Brea* decision, stating further, "The Administrator must show that such cases are processed with greater dispatch than they would otherwise receive or they risk dismissal under Rule 33."

The Brea case and its progeny gives us some insight as to how the Board looks at reasons for exceeding the six-month limit imposed by the Stale Complaint Rule. Another case that shows how the Board looks at this is *Administrator v. Merritt*, NTSB Order No. EA-3339, June 26, 1001. An ALJ had dismissed the Administrator's complaint that sought to suspend respondent Merritt's private pilot certificate because the FAA was late with the Notice of Proposed Certificate Action. Here, the FAA sent the notice by registered mail 11 days prior to the expiration of the six-month time limit imposed by Rule 33 of the Board. However, the pilot did not receive the notice until 17 days later, which made it six days after the time had run. The full Board reversed the ALJ's dismissal of the Administrator's complaint, maintaining that there was good cause for the delay since the notice was mailed in sufficient time prior to the six-month deadline and it could be reasonably assumed that it would be delivered before the time had run out. The Board said, "The Administrator should be able to plan and process his cases with the expectation that the postal service ordinarily will be able to deliver communications to airmen within a week or less." I don't know about a "week or less" the way the postal service has been working, but 17 days is a bit much, and the Board's decision seems to me to be quite reasonable. How about you?

As mentioned above, one of the exceptions that will circumvent the Stale Complaint Rule is the case of the alleged violator lacking the qualifications to hold the grade of certificate he has. However, the Board ruled in *Administrator v. Calder*, NTSB Order No. EA-3565, April 30, 1992, that merely alleging a lack of qualification is not sufficient. It must be proved.

In this case, in an obvious attempt to procedurally circumvent the Stale Complaint Rule, the FAA alleged a lack of qualification, and the Board saw right through it. Respondent Calder was charged with violation of the regulation regarding minimum altitudes. He was accused of flying an airship 150' to 300' above the ground, and that he was not carrying his airman certificate and his medical while doing so, as required by regulation. Since the complaint was brought well beyond the six-month time limit, it would certainly be stale if not for the allegation of lack of qualification.

Petitioner Calder filed a motion to dismiss on the basis that the complaint was stale, and the Administrator failed to timely answer this petition. Therefore, the law judge dismissed the complaint as stale. The Administrator appealed, and the full board, citing the previous case of *Administrator v. Rothbart and Voorhees*, NTSB Order No. EA-3052 (1990), reconsideration denied, NTSB Order No. EA-3356 (1991), affirmed the ALJ's decision to dismiss. The Board said, "we found that where a respondent's motion to dismiss raises the question of whether the Administrator is attempting to allege lack of qualifications as a device to avoid dismissal of a complaint under Rule 33. It is incumbent upon the Administrator to respond to the points made in support of respondent's position, and the Administrator's failure to do so leaves unchallenged the circumstances described in the motion to dismiss. In the instant case, the Administrator failed to timely respond, and when he did respond he failed to address any of respondent's substantive arguments - despite the fact that they necessarily raised the issue of whether the Administrator's allegation of lack of qualification was other than a procedural device. Moreover, because we find that it cannot be fairly stated that this complaint presents an issue of qualification, we conclude that the law judge did not abuse his discretion in dismissing the complaint."

In *Administrator v. Hawes*, NTSB Order No. EA-3830, March 9, 1993, the Board again affirmed the ALJ's dismissal of the Administrator's complaint as stale under Rule 33. In this case, the FAA revoked the inspection authorization of respondent Hawes for failure to properly inspect an aircraft.

Hawes appealed the revocation, complaining the complaint was stale. Therefore, in order to justify the revocation, the FAA amended the complaint to include language stating that respondent "lacked the degree of care, judgment, and responsibility" required of the holder of an inspection authorization. The main thrust of the Administrator's case was based on the exception to the stale complaint rule in the case of lack of qualification. The ALJ ruled in favor of Hawes, dismissing the complaint. The FAA appealed.

The Board affirmed the law judge's action, stating that, "where the sanction is revocation, the case of necessity involves a lack of qualification issue."

On the other hand, a legitimate case of lack of qualification will override the stale complaint rule, as shown by the case of *Administrator v. Walters*, NTSB Order No. EA-3835, March 16, 1993. In this one, respondent Walters was alleged by the Administrator to have made false entries on numerous past applications for medical certificates, failing to fully disclose his record of traffic convictions. The FAA revoked all his medical certificates and suspended his airman certificates for 60 days. Respondent Walters appealed, asking for dismissal of the complaint on the basis of Rule 33. The ALJ granted his request.

The FAA then appealed to the full Board, and the Board reversed the ALJ, holding, "The case now before us.... involves a legitimate issue of qualification arising from the Administrator's allegations that respondent made fraudulent or intentionally false statements on a series of medical applications. Such charges, if proven, would clearly provide a basis for sustaining the revocation of respondent's medical certificate. Consequently, the complaint in this case was not subject to dismissal under Rule 33, and the law judge thus erred in granting respondent's motion (for dismissal)."

That the Administrator does not necessarily have to prove that the respondent was notified of his proposed certificate action within the six months of the event as required by the stale complaint rule is demonstrated by *Administrator v. Davila-Ramos*, NTSB Order No. EA-3939, July 9, 1993. In this case the NOPCA was timely sent by registered mail, which was returned by the postal service as "unclaimed." The Administrator then sent another copy of the NOPCA by regular mail, which the respondent claimed to have never received. He therefore sought dismissal of the Administrator's complaint, pleading the Stale Complaint Rule. This plea fell on deaf ears, as the Board held that the mailing of the second notice constituted "constructive notice," therefore defeating the Stale Complaint Rule.

The Board had reached the same conclusion in *Administrator v. Coombs*, NTSB Order No. EA-3609, June 19, 1992. In this case, respondent Coombs admitted that he received the NOPCA in a timely fashion, but the revocation order was returned three times as "unclaimed" by the postal service when it was sent by certified mail. The order was then sent by regular mail and was not returned.

In the case of *Administrator v. Meuiner*, NTSB Order No. EA-4004, October 19, 1993, the Board held that the filing of respondent Meuiner's appeal one day late was cause for dismissal on the Administrator's motion -- even though the notice of appeal was filed a day before the deadline for filing. (Respondent claimed that since he had filed the notice of intent to appeal one day prior to the filing deadline, the time should be extended for an additional day.) In dismissing the appeal, the Board said, "We find no justification for respondent's error, for the applicable rule clearly states that the time

AN AERO-LEGAL RESOURCE GUIDE 149

for filing an appeal brief is five days after the notice of appeal is filed, not five days after the last day it could have been filed. Thus, whether viewed as an error of computation or of construction, it does not appear that the lateness of the brief is excusable for good cause shown."

As I mentioned above, there are exceptions to the Stale Complaint Rule. One of these is the situation where the sanction of revocation is applied to an airman based on a drug conviction. The exception of "lack of qualification to hold the certificate" is the rationale for this. In the case of *Administrator v. Beauchemin*, NTSB Order No. EA-4371, June 9, 1995, respondent Beauchamin had his pilot certificate revoked because he pled guilty to being engaged in a "continuing criminal enterprise", the importation and distribution of marijuana for economic gain. In appealing to the Board, respondent Beauchamin claimed that the FAA's complaint should have been dismissed because it was initiated more than six months after the FAA first became aware of his conviction, and thus, according to Rule 33, subject to dismissal as stale. In rejecting this argument, the Board said, "We have held that any conviction involving the sale of drugs, even if it does not involve the use of an aircraft, warrants revocation based on a lack of qualification." Lack of qualification has always been one of the exceptions to the Stale Complaint Rule, and the Board has applied this to revocation for drug offenses.

### More on Timing

In addition to the Stale Complaint Rule there are several other factors of timing that can affect the outcome of an enforcement case. In *Administrator v. Morse*, NTSB Order No. EA-3659, August 12, 1992, the Board granted an extension of the date of filing an appeal to the Board from an ALJ's decision, but denied the petitioner Morse's mistaken belief that he also was granted an extension. Both the Administrator's and the respondent's appeals were due on August 10. On the 7th, the attorneys for both sides discussed requesting an extension. The Administrator then requested an extension from the Board and was granted an extension from August 10 until August 24.

The FAA attorney confirmed this by letter to respondent Morse's counsel, who therefore believed that the extension applied to both parties. He then filed his appeal on August 21, and the Board refused to accept it, saying it was too late, having been due on the 10th. Respondent Morse's commercial pilot certificate and flight instructor certificate were revoked. In refusing to accept the late filing of the airman's appeal, the Board held that "Respondent's alleged reliance on opposing counsel's obtaining an extension for both cannot extend beyond receipt of the August 8 letter, because that letter may not reasonably be read to grant respondent an extension. At that point, counsel should have contacted the Board regarding any arguable misunderstanding. Respondent, however, took no action, instead choosing to wait even longer to file his brief, failing even to mention this matter until the motion to strike was filed. We do not find that these circumstances demonstrate good cause, under *Administrator v. Hooper*, NTSB Order No. EA-2781 (1988) to accept the late-filed appeal."

The case of *Administrator v. Prior*, NTSB Order No. EA-4469, July 17, 1996, is particularly interesting in that most actions filed with the Board are counted as of the date **sent** (the date of mailing), but in this case the Board dismissed the motion for a stay of the Board's Order of Suspension pending appeal to the US Circuit Court of Appeals because it was **received** three days late, although it was mailed timely.

### The Dreaded "609 Ride"

Nobody likes to have his or her competence questioned, particularly airpeople who have held their certificates for several years, but every pilot applicant is told at the time of issuance of a certificate that "the FAA giveth and the FAA can taketh away." In fact, right on the temporary certificate, among the "Conditions of Issuance" is the statement that the certificate becomes void, "Upon the refusal or failure by the holder to accomplish a flight check by a Flight Standards Inspector if so requested...." The implication is that at any time, for any (or no) reason, the FAA may require an airperson to demonstrate the knowledge and skill required of the holder of a certificate of the grade held. This authority to recheck airpeople is, however, not absolute. Not only must the Feds have a reason to demand such a reexamination, but it must be a valid (reasonable) reason. The "609 Ride" is frequently used as a means of checking an airperson's skill level after an accident, incident, or violation. Like the sanctions of suspension or revocation, it is considered remedial in nature rather than punishment, unlike the civil penalty (fine) imposed in some violation cases that is considered to be punishment. The nature of the re-examination (what is to be tested) is determined by the particular knowledge or skill of the airman that has been brought into question.

Both of these concepts are demonstrated by the case of *Administrator v. Wang*, NTSB Order No. EA-3264 March 1, 1991. Respondent Wang had taken off into IMC conditions (under IFR) without first obtaining a clearance to do so. He was invited to take an instrument flight check with an FAA Aviation Safety Inspector, "with emphasis on Federal Aviation Regulations and air traffic procedures." He refused to do so, and the Administrator issued an order suspending his private pilot certificate.

Respondent Wang appealed this order, claiming that re-examination was unnecessary because he knew a clearance was required and he in fact believed he had a clearance. The ALJ, siding with the Administrator, affirmed the order of suspension.

Wang then appealed to the full Board, which also affirmed, holding that: "In the context of this case, in which there appears to be no dispute that the failure to obtain a takeoff clearance for an IFR flight raises an issue as to the pilot's instrument competence, the Administrator, to establish a reasonable basis for his re-examination request, was obligated to show only that respondent took off in his aircraft without the necessary clearance, for there is no doubt that a re-examination would be appropriate for a pilot who did not know that he should have obtained a clearance. The Administrator thus was not obligated to prove that respondent intentionally took off without a clearance or to disprove the evidence that respondent thought he had been cleared. So long as lack of competence could have caused the incident, the Administrator's request for a re-examination cannot be deemed arbitrary, and the possibility that the incident was not caused by incompetence does not render the request unreasonable."

The case of *Administrator v. Evans*, NTSB Order No. EA-3432, November 8, 1991, is interesting for two reasons. First, it again demonstrates that the word of the FAA is worthless. (You may recall that in my own case the manager of the Detroit FSDO assured me, "The matter is closed. You'll hear no more about this." And four and one-half years later it was brought up to strip me of my designation as a pilot examiner). Secondly, it demonstrates that a successful "609 Ride" may be considered in determining an appropriate sanction. The facts of this one indicate that respondent Evans lost control of his airplane on take-off when he was caught by a gust of wind, causing "substantial damage" to the airplane. There were no injuries.

As a result of this accident, an FAA Inspector called in Evans for a re-examination. He took the ride and passed. He then received a letter stating that, "you may consider the matter is closed."

Despite this assurance, three months later respondent Evans received a Notice of Proposed Certificate Action, followed by an order suspending his pilot certificate for 60 days. Obviously the word of the FAA is worthless.

Acting in his own behalf and appearing *in pro per*, Evans appealed to the NTSB. Since his appeal failed to answer the charges, the allegations as to the facts were deemed to be admitted. The ALJ was limited only to a consideration of the appropriate sanction. Because respondent Evans had completed a successful re-examination, the ALJ determined that no sanction was warranted. The Administrator appealed to the full Board.

The Board, siding with the FAA, threw out the issue of "double jeopardy," but they went on to deny the FAA's appeal, stating, "We believe that the law judge could properly conclude that there was a likelihood that the incident resulted more from the severity of the wind conditions than from carelessness, and that this obviated the need for any form of suspension of respondent's private pilot certificate. The law judge's determination is not inconsistent with any Board precedent cited by the Administrator, and we will not, therefore, disturb his initial decision."

As pointed out earlier, the right of the Administrator to demand that an airman be re-examined is not absolute. Good cause must be shown. However, reason to believe that the original certificate was issued in error, or was otherwise not properly issued, is always cause to require reexamination.

In *Administrator v. Carson*, NTSB Order No, EA-3905, June 7, 1993, the Administrator had reason to believe that respondent Carson and another mechanic's certificates were issued based on incomplete examinations. Therefore, they were asked to submit to a re-examination under Section 609 of the Act. Both refused, claiming that they had earned the certificates, challenging the right of the Administrator to demand that they be rechecked. Both certificates were therefore suspended, and both airmen appealed.

The Agency contended that the Designated Mechanic Examiner who conducted the oral and practical examinations had failed to cover several of the subject areas required by the Aviation Mechanic Examiner Handbook. (The examiner's designation had been revoked, along with all his certificates).

There was no allegation that the airmen themselves were guilty of any wrongdoing, but the Board held that even so, their certificates were subject to suspension, saying, "We have repeatedly held that to prevail on an order suspending an airman certificate pending successful reexamination, the Administrator need only show that a reasonable basis exists for questioning the certificate holder's competence.... the additional burdens imposed on the respondents that requiring that they be retested do not outweigh the Administrator's interest in insuring that unqualified individuals not be allowed to perform maintenance on aircraft." Another interesting concept is brought out by the Board in its decision in the next case offered here for your consideration. It seems that neither a pilot's skill nor his or her judgment need be brought into question for the Administrator to require a re-examination.

In *Administrator v. Berg*, NTSB Order No. EA-3364, July 22, 1991, the Board held that regardless of his or her skill as an airperson, the Administrator may require a re-examination if he has reason to question that individual's competence. Respondent Berg had been cleared by the local controller in the tower to land on runway 31R, and he lined up for landing on 31C.

He was then told to "go around." Instead, he sidestepped over to execute an uneventful landing on 31R. The local FSDO invited him in for a "609 Ride" and he refused. His private pilot certificate was suspended pending his agreement to submit to re-examination. He appealed the suspension, maintaining that his actions did not demonstrate a lack of piloting ability. The Board ruled for the Administrator, saying, "the issue before us is not whether respondent's operation of his aircraft in fact demonstrated a lack of competence, either in his skill or judgment as a pilot, but whether a lack of competence could have been a causative factor... Since a lack of qualification or competence could have accounted for the incident, the Administrator is entitled to satisfy himself that they did not, without regard to respondent's views as to the necessity or utility of a re-examination to accomplish that result."

The fact that an airperson successfully completes a reexamination does not preclude the imposition of a sanction in the event of a violation. In the case of *Administrator v. Thomas*, NTSB Order No. EA-4309, December 14, 1994, the Board upheld the Administrator's 15-day suspension of respondent Thomas' pilot certificate even though the FAA incident report said, "incident closed with this report."

Thomas pled that he would not have cooperated with the investigation if he had not relied on that statement.

# Chapter 10

## Other Interesting Cases and Final Conclusions

## Careless or Reckless

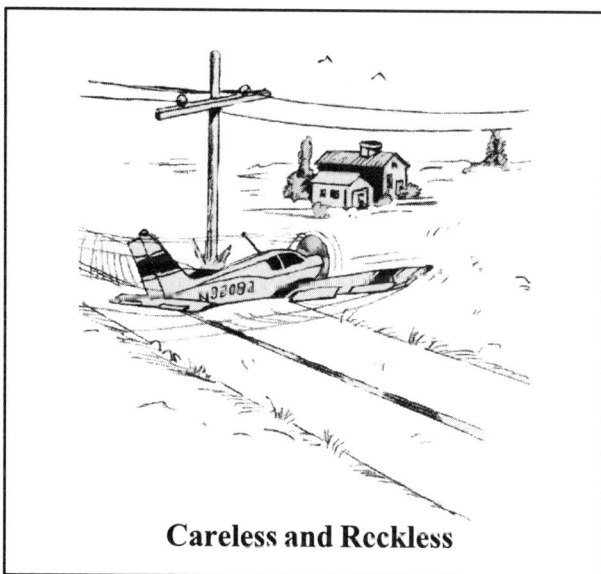

**Careless and Reckless**

Somehow the FAA seems to think that every accident, incident, or violation has to be the result of a careless or reckless act on the part of the pilot involved, for they almost invariably throw in a charge of violation of FAR 91.13 (formerly 91.9) along with the substantive charge or charges that may be appropriate. This is especially one that no airperson wants on his or her record so the Agency, particularly if they have a weak case, will sometimes throw it in as a bargaining chip to get the alleged violator to cave in and accept (without an appeal) whatever sanction the Agency is seeking if they agree to drop this one.

Although the Board will almost "rubber stamp" a charge of violation of 91.13 when it is offered as a residual or ancillary addition to another violation, when it stands alone as the sole charge against an airperson the Board is likely to dismiss when the Administrator fails to prove actual or potential endangerment. A case in point is that of *Administrator v. Westhoff*, NTSB Order No. EA-3596, June 3, 1992. This one demonstrates the Board's requirement that the Administrator must prove his case. A mere allegation is not sufficient.

The case was brought by the FAA because respondent Westhoff, an airline captain, had allowed the left main gear of his Boeing 727 to roll off the ramp into soft mud during a powerback from the gate. The wording of FAR 91.9 forbids operation of an aircraft" in a careless or reckless manner so as to endanger the life or property of another." The ALJ found for the FAA and upheld the charge because this was a commercial operation with passengers aboard and there was potential for endangerment.

The Board reversed and dismissed the charge, holding, "We do not agree with the law judge's conclusion that potential endangerment was established merely because this was a passenger-carrying flight. The likelihood that the passengers, who were already seated and belted in for take off, could have been injured during a powerback operation simply because the left main gear of the aircraft had slowly rolled off the edge of the ramp is far from self-evident, and, we think, absent any evidence on the matter, too remote to support a finding of a violation of FAR Section 91.9. In any event, we need not speculate as to what could have happened to the aircraft or its passengers under the circumstances presented. The burden was on the Administrator to establish that there was some likelihood of injury or damage by the introduction of substantial, reliable, and probative evidence. The Administrator failed to meet that burden here."

In another case, *Administrator v. Kapton*, NTSB Order No. EA-4046, December 13, 1993, the Board found respondent Kapton to be careless or reckless for failing to follow the procedures recommended in the **FAA Flight Training Manual**, which require an aircraft to have its main wheels chocked or the tail tied down with a qualified person at the controls and the brakes set when hand-propping an airplane.

Now compare these to NTSB Board member John J. Goglia's dissenting opinion in the case of *Administrator v. Nelson*, NTSB Order No. EA-4533, March 5, 1997. Here, he stated, "Under these circumstances it is unnecessary and illogical to find a violation of 91.13(a). There is **not** always a 'residual' violation of carelessness. A flight can be perfectly safe and a violation can nevertheless occur." Although this point was made in a dissenting opinion, it is certainly food for thought. Respondent Nelson had been charged with violation of FAR 91.119(a), (b), and (c), violation of minimum altitude requirements as he searched for a downed model glider in a Piper J3 Cub. The Administrator had automatically thrown in a charge of "careless and reckless" in violation of 91.13(a). Of this case, John Yodice, writing in the **LPBA Journal**, Spring 1997 issue, had this to say. "I have not seen another thoughtful analysis of this regulation since the dissent of Board Member Joseph Nail in *Administrator v. Hart* 6 NTSB 899, 903 (1988). The additional charge of carelessness has become so automatic as to make the regulation almost meaningless. It would be well for the full Board to address this issue."

The case of *Administrator v. Reynolds*, 4 NTSB 240 (1982), established the principle that in order to demonstrate endangerment the Administrator must show "either the likelihood of such an occurrence was unacceptably high, or that the pilot's exercise of judgment in the matter was clearly deficient." This, however, was a helicopter case, and the Board has gone out of the way to differentiate between helicopters and fixed wing aircraft in several more recent cases. As John Yodice put it, again writing in the **LPBA Journal**, Spring 1993, "In several more recent cases the Board has said *Reynolds* applies only to helicopter cases. In one case, a pilot was found negligent in taxiing a fixed wing aircraft too close to an individual signaling to try to stop the aircraft. *Administrator v. King*, NTSB Order No. EA-3861, April 26, 1993. In (an) other, two airline pilots were found negligent in taking off an airliner below take off minimums. *Administrator v. Erikson and Nehez*, NTSB Order No. EA-3869, April 30, 1993. The Board has gone so far as to say that 'as to fixed wing aircraft a violation of an operational regulation is sufficient to support a finding of a residual or derivative section 91.9 (now 91.13) violation' and no endangerment, not even potential, need be proven. The Board adds that a residual or derivative finding has no effect on sanction. *Administrator v. Haney*, NTSB Order No. EA-11047, March 15, 1993. The Board, egged on by the FAA, seems to be moving toward rendering a 'careless or reckless' charge meaningless."

### Good Moral Character

As far as the FAA is concerned, there are only two kinds of people who are required to have "good moral character" in order to hold airman certificates: the Airline Transport Pilot certificate and the Ground Instructor certificate. I personally know of more than one holder of one or another of these certificates who is of extremely bad moral character (including an FAA Aviation Safety Inspector), but I have never heard of anyone having a certificate revoked for lack of good moral character. I wonder just what one has to do to demonstrate a lack of this quality?

The case of *Administrator v. Neff*, NTSB Order No. EA-3920, June 18, 1993, demonstrates how the NTSB views this subject. Respondent Neff was convicted of failing to pay his income tax, and the FAA revoked his ATP certificate, asserting that this conviction demonstrated a lack of good moral character and therefore he was not qualified to hold the certificate. (We know that lack of qualification is cause for revocation.)

Neff maintained that he refused to pay his income tax as a matter of principle. The Board ruled against the FAA and in favor of respondent Neff, saying, "that where, as in the circumstances of this case, such conduct, however unlawful it may be held or viewed to be, flows from a genuine objection to the validity of the tax sought to be collected, it will not support a finding that the objecting party lacks good moral character."

Again, in *Administrator v. Saunders*, NTSB Order No. EA-3672, August 29, 1992, the Board found for the airman, this time because the FAA failed to prove its case by a "preponderance of the evidence." The FAA had charged Saunders with several violations and sought to revoke his ATP pilot certificate and medical certificate claiming a lack of good moral character, based on a Florida conviction of indecent exposure. The Board held that the Administrator had failed to demonstrate that respondent Saunders lacked good moral character by a preponderance of the evidence, saying, "Respondent was convicted of one count of indecent exposure under a statute that encompasses both exposure 'in a public place or in the private premises of another, or so near thereto as to be seen from such private premises.' 800.03 Florida Statutes. There is no indication that this was other than a first offense. Respondent was directed to perform community service, and placed on a year's probation, in lieu of incarceration or fine. The only inkling in the record of the circumstances of the offense is the direction in the judge's order, not to go to a specified address. This suggests that the incident occurred on private property. The Administrator has the burden of proving his case, and must do so by a preponderance of the evidence. He has offered absolutely no information concerning the incident, perhaps believing that, on its face, it establishes a lack of good moral character. We cannot find that, as a matter of law, what has been presented to us by way of evidence is adequate to find lack of good moral character so as to require revocation of respondent's ATP. The proof does not rise near the level discussed in *Roe*. (*Administrator v. Roe*, 45 CAB 969, 1968.) While it may well be that, should the circumstances be known they would support the finding sought by the Administrator, we cannot find on the evidence before us, as *Roe* dictates, that respondent has complete disregard for the rights of other human beings. Nor can we find on this record (as we did in *Roe*) that respondent has such character deficiencies that he represents a threat to safety in air transportation. Accordingly, we find that the Administrator has not met his burden of proving that respondent does not meet the good moral character requirement of Section 61.151."

Saunders got to keep his certificates. The language of this decision sounds to me as though the Board was sending a message to the FAA legal staff: **"Do your homework, fellows!"**

The implication is that if the FAA Associate General Counsel had been better prepared, with an account of the incident resulting in the conviction of indecent exposure, the outcome might well have been different.

### Reduction of Sanction Because of
### Attainment of Higher Grade Certificate

There have been several cases in which the alleged violator obtained a higher grade of certificate between the time of the alleged violation and the imposition of the order of sanction by the FAA, and this factor may or may not have an influence on the sanction itself. The *Bennett* case is interesting, not only for this reason, but because both the ALJ and the Board enunciated several other principles of interest. In *Administrator v. Bennett*, NTSB Order No. EA-3429, November 4, 1991, respondent Bennett was the subject of an emergency order revoking his **student** pilot certificate for carrying a passenger. However, at the suggestion of an FAA inspector, he had obtained his **private** pilot certificate by the time the FAA issued the order.

In compliance with this order, to surrender his student certificate, respondent Bennett surrendered his private certificate. Realizing that the respondent had upgraded his certificate, the FAA amended the order to call for a 180-day suspension rather than revocation as would be appropriate for a student carrying a passenger. Bennett appealed, pleading, among other things that he was out of pocket some $28,000 for removal and repairs to the crashed airplane. In further reducing the sanction from a 180-day suspension to only 45 days, the ALJ held that his expenses constituted a "clear and compelling" reason for the reduction. As an aside, he also noted, that the Board has, "been inundated with these emergency cases" that require accelerated procedures and interfere with the normal docket of cases.

The ALJ, leaning a sympathetic ear to this plea, reduced the sanction to a 45-day suspension of the private certificate. The FAA appealed to the full Board, which reversed the ALJ and reinstated the 180-day suspension.

Contrary to the ALJ's finding, the Board found no "clear and compelling" reason for the additional reduction of sanction to 45 days, stating, "The law judge's further reduction is predicated on... the economic impact on the respondent and his business of the expenses associated with the retrieval, repair, and the loss of use of his aircraft. We (do not see this) circumstance as justifying any reduction in sanction."

### Let's Make Up Our Own Rules

Frequently an inspector will decide to take some action based on a nonexistent regulation. In the majority of these instances it is ignorance that causes the problem. In his or her ignorance, the inspector doesn't know that there is no rule covering the situation so s/he assumes there is and takes action.

The most blatant example of ignorance on the part of an FAA inspector taking inappropriate action is the infamous case in which an inspector grounded a flock of airplanes with "Q-tip" props on the mistaken belief that they were all damaged by prop strikes. The guy was unfamiliar with Q-Tip props.

However, even though most of this business of making up their own regulations is the result of ignorance, there is some of this that springs from deliberate viciousness. Way back in the introduction, I mentioned the three kinds of inspectors one finds in Flight Standards: The vast majority, who are merely putting in their time until they can draw their pensions; the second, smaller group comprised of a bunch of power-mad individuals who, given a little authority, throw their weight around at the expense of the flying public, and, finally, that very small group of dedicated public servants.

An example of the Napoleon type is seen in the case of Mike Taylor, in which Inspector DiMartini got Taylor convicted of violating rules that don't even exist. By the bye, on that same subject of viciousness, that same Inspector DiMartini is alleged to have threatened a helicopter operator and pilot with bringing an army of maintenance inspectors to tear his helicopter apart until they found something wrong with it. This, after it was pointed out to him that he was citing nonexistent regulations. It seems that this guy DiMartini has a personal agenda and creates regulations to fit. He is certainly not the only inspector who engages in this practice. The inspector who, knowing the regulations nonetheless substitutes his/her own ideas may be likened to a traffic cop stopping a motorist for going 45 m.p.h. in a 55 zone because the cop believed the statute should be 45.

Many of these cases of inspectors making up their own rules are most apparent during random ramp checks. The infamous Q-tip prop situation was the most widely publicized, and that inspector was sent back for more training. These ramp check mistakes are most likely to occur in the case of somewhat unusual or uncommon aircraft. The owner of an AT-6 who regularly performs in airshows found four FAA inspectors crawling all over his airplane at a CAF show. They had the canopy open and were looking inside when the owner found them. He ordered them off under threat of having them forcibly removed by the local police. They demanded to know if the parachute was current and were informed that it had been repacked at Oshkosh. They then wanted to know, "When was Oshkosh?" On another occasion, at a different airshow, an inspector demanded that the owners/operators of all the AT-6s produce logbook evidence of current annual inspections under threat of grounding all the airplanes until such evidence was produced. Since none of the airplanes were based at that location, none of the owner/operators had the aircraft logs with them.

Unlike a pilot certificate and medical that must be carried on the pilot's person when exercising his privileges, the aircraft maintenance records must be produced "on reasonable notice", a fact of which that inspector was apparently unaware.

I was once personally asked by an ignorant inspector to describe the hydraulic system on a Beech Model 18. He was looking for the gear system; the only hydraulics on that model airplane are on the brakes! And I recently learned of an inspector who asked the operator of a turbine-powered helicopter where the carb heat control was located.

Finally, at another airshow, an inspector grounded a Beechcraft Model 17 (an old Beech Staggerwing) because it lacked an MEL (Minimum Equipment List). Bear in mind, at the time the airplane was manufactured MELs were not even in existence, and such a document would not have been required in any event.

### Conclusions

Please understand that the cases I've cited here are truly representative of the NTSB's thoughts. They have been selected to illustrate various points, but there's nothing unusual about them. In light of all that has been covered here, several important conclusions can be drawn. Because of the fact that FAA enforcement actions are administrative in nature rather than criminal, the burden on the Administrator to prove his case is much lighter, and the rules of evidence are much more lax.

Therefore, the cards are stacked heavily in favor of the agency and against the airperson. Even so, there shines an occasional glimmer of hope. If the airperson does his or her homework and is thoroughly prepared, he or she can actually prevail on occasion.

Just as is the case with automobile traffic ordinances, the vast majority of FAR violations go undetected. However, those that do come to the attention of the FAA are likely to encounter a solid wall in the implacable attitude of many of the people in the agency. The only way to deal with this is to make them prove every single point. As mentioned earlier, any attempt at cooperation is interpreted as a sign of weakness and only serves to encourage them to push harder. A perfect case in point is the Taylor matter, comprehensively covered in Chapter 2.

We have seen how some of the power-mad little people in the bureaucracy somehow believe that if they can bring down a particularly prominent airman it will somehow increase their own stature. Quite the contrary, this only serves to diminish them in the eyes of the flying public, indeed in the eyes of the public at large, increasing the contempt in which the agency is held. It is a wonder that the top brass in the FAA doesn't wake up and see what the resultant bad publicity is doing to the agency.

It is certainly understandable that the agency did what it did in the Phillips case, but it is indeed regrettable that they folded up and surrendered. Had they not done so, Darryl Phillips would have shown them for what they are. It is literally unbelievable that nobody in the FAA knows the difference between a post office box and a rural route box number. And how about the fact that the airman registry contains a substantial number of pilots with Spanish surnames with post office boxes in Miami? Had Darryl been able to get these facts on the record it could have been brought to the attention of the Inspector General for the Department of Transportation and even the Congress of the United States and ultimately benefited us all.

# APPENDICES

To: FAA Western Regional Manager
Bill "Withycombe" admin.tc.faa.gov

Dear Mr. Withycombe, Jan 15, 1998

Yesterday I received your letter concerning my FOIA. There are several items I feel I have a right to receive without any cost to me. Also I need some clarification regarding your final denial. Is this Tsuda's denial of information?

But first, I would like you to understand why this request was made. I assume you are a man of character and integrity. Certainly being employed by the FAA does not entitle you to that quality but hopefully one does not acquire you responsibility without some integrity. I apologize for any resentment but I believe you will understand why after you review my experience with your agency.

Please read the attachments to this letter. In those attachments there is a brief description of my experience. I am a former airline pilot and instructor. Almost three years ago I was confronted with an unusual training situation. What to do? Call the FSDO seemed the logical step. I did. A former 1000 hour Navy pilot, 6 year FAA air traffic, former instructor for McDonnell Aircraft training F-18 pilots, and currently Senior Safety Analyst for the Navy writing training lessons for the Navy (including navigation) approached me and asked me to help him get his FAA private license. I suggested he attend a ground school course I taught. He did.

FSDO instructions to me: Since his actual military time was more than two years ago he would have to: 1) take the appropriate FAA written and 2) pass a checkride. FAR 61.41 applied. This sounded very reasonable. After attending my ground school he passed his written with 90+%. After flying several hours with him and checking him in 61.87 and 61.93 I signed him off to solo. I did not sign him off for x/c because I had not checked his planning, Wx, airports, etc., until the Friday evening before and the Sat.

morning of his x/c. At that time I endorsed his logbook for solo x/c. (The NTSB Final order states that it is a violation to endorse a logbook without FLYING WITH THE PILOT THE SAME DAY. (I have yet to find an instructor that agrees.). Additional instructions were given to pilot : Day VFR and refuel at destination.

Pilot failed to refuel as instructed requiring an emergency landing 18 miles short of home airport. Appropriate notification to FAA and NTSB.

During the investigation Inspector DeMartini first accused me of not completing 2 hour x/c required by FARs. When I attempted to explain, he said he did not care what happened. He was not interested in safety and was not out to prevent accidents but to find violations and I would be violated regardless. Immediately, I contacted his supervisor, Alan Hasquest, requesting another inspector. He informed me that I would have to work with DeMartini. However, he requested another inspector's opinion of the violation (Simon Wheaton-Smith). Wheaton-Smith wrote a two page letter explaining in his opinion there was no violation. This was subsequently sent to Tsuda. HENCE MY FOIA REQUEST FOR THAT LETTER. I do have tape recorded telephone conversation with FSDO describing the contents of this letter and that it was sent to Tsuda.

Continuing with DeMartini. After his threat and a call to Hasquest I called AOPA. I was assured the 2 hour x/c country was not a requirement for x/c. Advice given to me at that time was simple, you will eventually get a letter ending investigation DO NOT TALK TO FAA (from AOPA). The longer it takes the better.

Nine months later I get Tsuda's letter stating a violation of 61.93 C 1 I (reading aeronautical charts and nav.). DeMartini never asked about that or even suggested that was part of the violation. He never asked me or the pilot. That part of training was explained at the NTSB hearing and verified by the pilot. DeMartini then proceeds to manufacture a flight that I was never given a chance to explain 100% speculation. You must read the transcripts to begin to understand how absurd his testimony. Examples 5 minutes for 2 steep turns, 10 minutes for 3 stalls, 40 minutes for 3 touch and goes (done at 3 farm strips within 1 mile of each other). This was all information presented and never investigated. Did I get a fair chance to present this at the NTSB hearing what do you think??

Back to the Tsuda letter.
The Tsuda letter stated I may not have receive a letter dated 3 months ago. The sanction was a 3 month suspension of my CFI. I couldn't believe what I was reading. I contacted a lawyer and Jackie Clow of the FAA I had met when I was a Check airman at Eastern Airlines. I faxed her the information I sent DeMartini including information regarding an AOPA checklist that contained a checklist verifying Dead Reckoning and Pilotage (maps) completed on the last instruction flight signed and dated by both the pilot and myself. It is obvious why Tsuda did not want that packet part of the hearing record. Fact: she had it at the hearing waving it in front of my face during my testimony. Fact: DeMartini ignored that information during his investigation. Fact: I did not identify or discuss that document with DeMartini because his accusation was 2 hour x/c. Jackie Clow met with Tsuda a few days after I faxed her the information. I am amazed that Tsuda denies that information she made reference to in NTSB Hearing record April 95, SE 14730 (page 92 line 16-22) . Upon my comment that I sent the same information to DeMartini she immediately changed the line of questions to C-10 a totally different topic. HENCE, MY FOIA REQUEST FOR THAT INFORMATION.

I feel it is very unethical for an attorney to use a document during a hearing and then deny knowing any thing about it when requested by FOIA.

Another issue of my FOIA request is the basis for Inspector DeMartini's NTSB testimony (Pg 43 line 5-14) stating that the FAR 61.41 doesn't mean what it says. How can an FAR be dismissed without some legal basis? If this is the policy of the FAA any FAR could be dismissed simply because an inspector says so. HENCE MY FOIA REQUEST FOR THAT INFORMATION.

FAR 61.41 "Flight Instruction may be credited toward the

requirements for a pilot certificate .......if received from an Armed Force of the United States ....."

This pilot was a Navy pilot! When questioned before x/c flight the SDL FSDO did say this FAR did apply. My phone records show the 4 minute call to SDL FSDO before the x/c flt.

Other amazing events: 1) About a week after the NTSB hearing I was selected as one of the flight instructors of the year for the same FSDO during this same time period??? 2) Further evidence indicates the LA FAA office incorrectly addressed their NOPCA letter. I never received it. 3) When I attempted to defend myself the FAA increased the sanction against me suspending my private, commercial, ATP, FE, and A&P. How can that be justified?? 4) The FAA requested and succeeded in preventing the NTSB from reading their own report identifying the probable cause: "as pilots failure to refuel'" NOT A FAILURE IN NAVIGATION. Incidentally this information was never made available to me or the pilot. I eventually researched it on the INTERNET and found the report. Why would this report not be sent to the pilot and instructor involved. When a cause to TWA 800 is determined will TWA be notified??? 5) When DeMartini manufactured the last training flight totally by speculation 3 eyewitnesses that saw us do the touch and goes on farm strips were stricken from the record by the FAA and NTSB. Does this sound like a search or investigation that is concerned with facts???

And finally the character of Inspector DeMartini. I have requested several sources to investigate this inspector. Recently, I have received several complaints regarding DeMartini's unethical and abusive use of his authority. I am not alone in being harassed and terrorized by DeMartini. Several pilots have contacted me with similar stories, false accusations, FARs misrepresented and taken out of context and disregard for any information that might help explain a situation. I will be glad to share that information with you in further correspondence. Senator McCain is already in possession of this information if you would like to contact him..

DeMartini was eventually encouraged to leave the Portland area and has now been encouraged to leave the Scottsdale area. Watch out Van Nuys. I hear this is his next victim. It is certainly easier to pass on you problem rather than deal with it. I have requested numerous sources to investigate. I started with Kinney, Thomas, Hinson, Daschle, Valentine, Garvey, 1 800 for sure, numerous elected officials and as many FAA and government employees as possible.

Mr. Withycombe this is wrong and I will not live my remaining years questioning whether or not I should stand for truth and integrity. Currently, I am a High School Principal and face enthusiastic young adults almost everyday promoting mainstream American values of honesty, integrity and justice. I find it very difficult knowing that an agency of my government acts in such an irresponsible manner.
Please read attachments for further info.

Sincerely,
M Taylor

---

My response to Mike Taylor's letter follows:

Dear Mike:

I got the copy of your letter to Withycombe, and with your kind permission I will uses it in my book. My wife always said I have to be the most naive over fifty-year old man allowed to wander around at liberty because I always believe the best of people until they prove me wrong.
Like you, I had thought that above the bottom level the higher-ups in the FAA were people of integrity. Boy! Was I ever disillusioned! I was lied to by the regional manager (Great Lakes Region) and even the National Flight Standards Manager. These people are totally devoid of honor.
You should also know that a request for information under the FOIA will sometimes get one nowhere with the FAA. They just stall and stonewall apparently hoping that the request will be forgotten.

In my own case, they only provided my attorney and me with a few carefully selected documents, claiming that the rest of the file no longer existed.

As to my opinion of your letter, it is absolutely great. It will do no good, but it certainly lays out the story.

We have had two inspectors in our district that are just like DeMartini - they make up their own regulations to fit their personal agenda.

Unfortunately, the FAA closes ranks around them and protects their own.

Once again, I want to thank you for sharing that letter with me.

Warmest regards,

Howard

---

### List of Exhibits that Darryl Phillips
### never got to enter into evidence

1. Oklahoma Drivers License showing his home address
2. Voter Registration Card, showing his home address
3. UPS Shipping Label, showing delivery to his home address
4. Records from Airman Certification Branch, showing numerous pilots with actual Post Office Box numbers as their addresses

# Glossary

**Airport Traffic Area:** Five statute mile area around an airport with an operating control tower, up to, but not including 3000' above ground level

**AD Note:** Mandatory Airworthiness Directive requiring compliance by one means or another within a specified time

**Administrator:** Head honcho at the FAA

**ALJ:** Administrative Law Judge

**AME:** Aviation Medical Examiner (Doctor authorized to administer aviation physical examinations and issue medical certificates to airmen)

**ARSA:** Airport RADAR Service Area

**ASI:** Aviation Safety Inspector

**ASRP:** Aviation Safety Reporting Program

**ASRS:** Aviation Safety Reporting System (same as above)

**Associate General Counsel:** FAA Attorney

**Board:** The National Transportation Safety Board

**CAA:** Civil Aviation Authority (Predecessor of the FAA)

**CFR:** Code of Federal Regulations (Title 14 embodies the Aviation regulations, commonly referred to as the FARs)

**EAJA:** Equal Access to Justice Act (under which an airperson may recover the costs of successfully defending him/herself against the FAA)

**FAA:** Federal Aviation Administration; "The Agency"

**FAR:** Federal Air Regulations

**FOIA:** Freedom of Information Act

**FSDO:** Flight Standards District Office (The original bad guys)

**IFR:** Instrument Flight Rules

**IMC:** Instrument Meteorological Conditions

**LOI:** Letter of Investigation

**LSO** Landing Safety Officer

**NASA:** National Aeronautics and Space Administration

**NOPCA:** Notice of Proposed Certificate Action

**NTSB:** National Transportation Safety Board

*Pro Se:* (also *Pro per*) Proper person (one who represents himself in a legal matter, who acts as his own lawyer)

**TCA:** Terminal Control Area

**TRSA:** Terminal RADAR Service Area

**VFR:** Visual Flight Rules

**VMC:** Visual Meteorological Conditions

## CURRICULUM VITAE

## Howard J. Fried

348 Woodfield Square Lane
Brighton, MI 48116-4319
(810) 225 0421
Fax (810) 225 0567

## EDUCATION

AB (English) Western Reserve University 1948
BS (Psychology) Western Reserve University 1949
MA (Sociology) Western Reserve University 1950
Juris Doctor Wayne State University 1968*

Lecturer and Speaker on Aviation Education and Safety
Author of numerous articles on aviation training and safety
Author of three published books on matters aeronautical
Former (seven years) contributing editor – *FLYING*
Columnist for **Avweb**, the Internet aviation magazine
Expert witness in aviation litigation
1993 Honoree in International Forest of Friendship

## AVIATION EXPERIENCE

1. Trained in the military (U.S. Army Air Corps – World War II)

2. In excess of forty thousand hours of flight experience in all types of General Aviation airplanes, both normally aspirated and turbocharged as well as several turbo props and jets.

3. From 1968 until the present operate a very active flight school-training pilots for all certificates and ratings.

4. Cessna Aircraft Operations School 1976 (Factory School)

5. Beechcraft Factory School on the BE-60 (Duke)

6. Piper Factory School on the 601P (Pressurized Aerostar) 1985

7. Factory School on the Turbo Commander Model 690 1989

8. FAA Pilot examiner Training Program from its inception in 1978 through 1993.

9. Citation (CE500-550) Initial Training Program – Flight Safety International 1997

10. FAA Accident Prevention Counselor from the inception of the program in 1970 through 1993

## FAA CERTIFICATES AND RATINGS

Airline Transport Pilot – Airplane Single and Multiengine Land
Commercial Privileges – Airplane Single Engine Sea and Glider
Certified Flight Instructor – Airplanes Single and Multiengine Gliders
Instrument – Airplane

Ground Instructor – Advanced and Instrument

*Note: I took and passed the Michigan Bar, but have never practiced law.*

**UNITED STATES OF AMERICA**
NATIONAL TRANSPORTATION SAFETY BOARD
OFFICE OF ADMINISTRATIVE LAW JUDGES

                          SERVED FEB 13, 1998
                          CERTIFIED MAIL, RRR
************************************************
GROVER CLEVELAND CROCKER        *
**APPLICANT**                       *
                                *
V                               *
                                *
ADMINISTRATOR                   *
FEDERAL AVIATION ADMINISTRATION *
               RESPONDENT        *
************************************************

SERVICE:

Glenn Brown, Esq.
FAA/Alaskan Region
222 W. 7th, #14
Anchorage, AK 99513-7687

R. R. De Young, Esq.
Wade & De Young
4041 E. St. #200
Anchorage, AK

## DECISION AND ORDER

Pursuant to the Equal Access to Justice Act
(EAJA), 3 USC 594, et seq., and the National
Transportation Safety Board's rules implementing
the EAJA, 49 CFR 826.1, et seq., hereafter referred
to as Board's rules, this applicant comes before
the National Transportation Safety Board (the

board) for an award of attorney fees and other expenses in the amount of $42,231.46 against the Federal Aviation Administration (FAA), an agency of the United States. The Application was filed by Mr. Grover Cleveland Crocker through Counsel. The Application and supporting documents filed by the Applicant establish that he meets the eligibility requirements set out in the EAJA and Sec. #24.4 of the Board's rules. The Applicant was timely filed and procedurally correct.

## STATEMENT OF THE CASE

This EAJA action arises from an Emergency Order of Revocation issued by the FAA on April 11, 1997, revoking the Applicants Airline Transport Pilot (ATP) Certificate and Flight Instructor Certificate for a period of one year. The Order of Revocation alleged a regulatory violation of Federal Aviation Regulation alleged (FAR) section 61.99(a)(1), which states that

"No person may make or cause to be made any fraudulent or intentionally false statement on any application for a certificate, rating, or duplicate thereof issued under Part 61 of the Federal Aviation Regulations."

It was the Administrators allegation that on or about August 30, 1996, the Applicant here and respondent originally was presented with two applications for 1A Jet type ratings (FAA Form 8710-1). The forms were presented to the application by Mr. Michael A Spisak and Mr. Alan G Larson, both of whom the Applicant proceeded to examine. During and/or at the conclusion of the examination, various entries were made on the aforementioned forms. These entries included approval for the application and the subsequent issuance of temporary airman certificates (which included 1A jet type ratings) to Mr. Spisak and Mr. Larson. Ultimately, it was the Administrator's allegations that both these documents and the statements made therein by the Applicant were intentionally false and therefore in regulatory violation of FAR 61.59(a)(1).

In response, while the Respondent generally admitted to most of the allegations made by the Administrator, Respondent specifically denied every allegation, assertion and legal conclusion contained in the complaint in the regard that he made a fraudulent or intentionally false statement in the applications.

## THE PREVAILING PARTY REQUIREMENT

Section 824.1 of the Board's Rules provides that "An eligible party may receive an award when if prevails over the Federal Aviation Administration (FAA), unless the government's position in the proceeding was substantially justified or special circumstances make an award unjust." The Oral Initial Decision and Order entered in this case on May 16, 1997 ruled for this Applicant and reversed the FAA's Order of revocation. The Oral Initial Decision and Order was appealed by the FAA on May 19, 1997. On June 26, 1997, the Board, after finding no merit to the arguments advanced in the Administrator's appeal, formed an Opinion and Order denying the Administrator's appeal and affirming the initial decision. **Administrator v. Crocker.** NTSB Order No. EA 4565, Page 2. Accordingly the extreme of the underlying proceeding in final and the Applicant is the prevailing party.

There were no special circumstances that would make an award of attorney fees unjust. Therefore, the remaining issue is whether or not the FAA's position was substantially justified.

## SUBSTANTIAL JUSTIFICATION

An agency is not required to pay attorney fees or expenses where its position was substantially justified or where special circumstances make an award unjust. ( 5 U.B.C., Sec. 504(a)(1). To establish "substantial justification," the Government must "show (1) that there is a reasonable basis in truth for the facts alleged in the pleadings: (2) that there exists a reasonable basis in law for the theory it {the Government} propounds: and (3) that the facts alleged will reasonably support the legal theory advanced." McCrary v. Administrator. S NTSB 1235, 1238,(1986), citing United States v. 2116 Boxes of Bones Beef, 726 F.2d 1431 (10th Ctr. 1935). Further, the Administrator must be substantially justified at each step of the proceedings Alabin v. National Transportation Safety Board, 839 F. 2d s17 (D.C. Cir. 1988).

In the instant case, the law (61.59)(a)(1)) reasonably supports the suspension sought. However, the facts do not reasonably support the legal theory advanced. The Emergency Order of Revocation (OK) which revoked Applicant's Air Transport Pilot (ATP) Certificate alleged that Mr. Michael Spisak, who held an ATP Certificates, and Mr. Alan Larson, who also held an ATP Certificate, presented their applications (FAA Form 8716-1, exhibits C-4 and C-5) to the applicant, Mr. Crocker, for an IA-Jet rating on August 30, 1996, at Love Field in Dallas, Texas. The OR further alleges that during and/or at the conclusion of examination of Spisak and Larson,

> (a) A check mark indicating you had personally reviewed the applicant's pilot logbook, and that you were certifying that the individual met the pertinent requirements of FAR 61 for the pilot

certificate or rating sought.

(b) A check mark indicating you had personally tested and/or verified the applicant in accordance with pertinent procedures and standards.

(c) The number "4.1" in the block indicating the duration of the ground portion of the test.

(d) The number "1.6" in the block indicating the duration of the flight portion of the test.

And as to Larson:

(a) A check mark indicating you had personally tested and/or verified the applicant in accordance with pertinent procedures and standards.

(b) A check mark indicating you had personally tested and/or verified the applicant in accordance with pertinent procedures and standards.

(c) The number "4.0" in the block indicating the duration of the ground portion of the test.

(d) The number "1.6" in the block indicating the duration of the flight portion of the test.

The evidence at the hearing developed that the Fairbanks, Alaska Flight Standards District Office (FSDO) had an ongoing investigation involving Mr. Larson and Mr. Spisak at the time of the flight tests were given by Mr. Crocker on August

30, 1996. The San Antonio FSDO was the supervising FSDO of Mr. Crocker's designated pilot examiner (DPE) Certificate. In September, questions were raised by the Fairbanks FSDO with the San Antonio FSDO about the FAA Forms 8730-1 (Airman Certificate and/or Rating Application) that were prepared by Mr. Crocker for Mr. Spisak and Mr. Larson. (TR-549) (Exhibits C-4 - C-6). As a result, the San Antonio FSDO suspended Mr. Crocker's DPE certificate pending an investigation. By letter dated November 4, 1996 (Exhibit R-7), Mr. Crocker was advised by the San Antonio FSDO that the investigation did not establish a sufficient basis to withhold his DPE Certificate and it was reinstated. The evidence further developed that Mr. Crocker had never met Mr. Spisak or Mr. Larson prior to the day prior to the flight check. The evidence established that Mr. Crocker was a decorated and retired USAF pilot and a retired employee of the FAA after 24 years. (Exhibit R-34).

Notwithstanding the decision of the San Antonio FSDO concerning these flight tests, the Fairbanks FSDO advised the operations supervisor of the San Antonio FSDO that they believed there were still two problem areas with the flight tests; use of a group oral exam and the actual amount of time used for the tests. (TR 336 and 239). As a result, the applicant's DPE was again suspended by the San Antonio FSDO (Exhibits R-8) and the investigation seems to have been, at that time, turned over to the Fairbanks FSDO.

What is critical to this EAJA decision is that the time issue raised by the Fairbanks FSDO, after the reinstatement letter of November 4, 1996 had been considered and reviewed by the San Antonio FSDO prior to the issuance of that reinstatement letter. This group oral issue was quickly dispelled by Mr. Crocker when he pointed out to the San Antonio FSDO that the FAA publications permitted this procedure. (TR-239).

The first discrepancy noted in both applications was the entry indicating that Mr. Crocker had looked at both Mr. Spisak's and Mr. Larson's log books. The problem here for the Administrator, and was pointed out by Mr. Crocker throughout these proceedings, was that the form only provided for the log book entry, but the regulations provided that the DPE could review the logbook or other training record (TR -283), which is what Mr. Crocker did and he so advised the Administrator at the onset. Mr. Crocker was in full compliance with the regulations. There was no substantial justification for the Administrator to pursue this allegation.

The other three allegations as to each application related directly to the time involved for the exam. At each stage of the proceedings, Mr. Crocker attempted to explain his time and procedure that the explanation was accepted by his supervisory FSDO (Exhibit R-7). But still the Fairbanks FSDO, several thousand miles away, pressed on. The case was tried by the FAA Counsel from Anchorage, Alaska, instead of local FAA Regional Counsel. FAA Counsel stated in his opening statement that "Our one true expert" would testify that the time involved was not sufficient to have completed the requirements of the test. When that expert was called, he related that he had participated in over 5,000 events associated with the issuance of a type rating and 180 to 200 events in a Jet Commander. (TR -341) This expert, Mr. Andrews, then later testified that in these 5,900 events he had never tested two applicants at the same time. (TR-353) (Emphasis added)

The key to the time issue throughout this case, and particularly as testified to by Mr. Spisak, Mr. Robin Smith and Mr. Crocker was the organization and precision that Mr. Crocker had developed over many years in administrating these check rides to dual applicants. Mr. Crocker's other witnesses also testified to this precision. As testified to, the primary reason for this precision was the huge operating expense of this particular aircraft and the necessity of completing the check ride in the shortest possible time.

In this regard, the Administrator's "one true expert" had no expertise at all in the most critical aspect of this case.

The most important quote relative to the time issue was stated by Mrs. Geiger, the Operations Unit Supervisor who initially reinstated Mr. Crocker's DPE Certificate, who said that "If it was too small a number (time involved), <u>it would possibly indicate that it was not a valid test</u>. " (TR-192) (Emphasis added) The Administrator's evidence throughout this proceeding when considered in its best light, might have indicated a possible invalid test and this evidence was all circumstantial. There was no evidence, direct or circumstantial, of intentional falsification, except in the inference the Administrator sought from the possible invalid test. Circumstantial evidence on the issue of intentional falsification "must be so compelling that no other determination is possible." Administrator v. Hart, EA 950 (January 1977, at page 24).

Mr. Crocker put on several witnesses that all testified to his truth and veracity and in the rebuttal, on of the Administrator's witnesses disputed Mr. Crocker's reputation for truth and veracity but could only testify that Mr. Crocker had a reputation for being easy with his examination. Just as a reputation for being easy has no relationship to dishonesty (intentional falsification), neither does a possibly invalid test indicate intentional falsification.

Therefore, the Administrator was not substantially justified for each step of the proceedings and the applicant is entitled to recover his fees under the EAJA.

## AWARD AMOUNT

In litigating this matter, the applicant has incurred $37,482 in legal fees. This amount is based on 181.6 at $120.00 per hour (attorney rate), 57.6 hours at $94.00 hour (law clerk rate), and 234.6 hours at $60 per hour (legal assistant rate). With more than 430 hours of billable time expended in this matter, such hours require the undersigned to take a closer look at the nature and reasonableness of the time expended. Under the EAJA, a prevailing party can only be awarded for the time that is reasonably expended on the matter. Brown v. Bashke 588 F.2d 634,637 (1978). After a thorough review of all applicable documents and supporting records, it is the undersigned's conclusion that under the circumstances the amount of time billed for this matter is excessive and unreasonable for the following reasons and shall be adjusted accordingly.

First, the Administrator filed the complaint to this matter on April 11, 1997. Thus, all fees and expenses incurred prior to that date were not fees and expenses incurred in to an adversary adjudication and thus are not recoverable under the EAJA. Peterson v. Administrator NTSB Order No. EA-4490 at 8. Accordingly, the billable hours for attorney's fees will be reduced by 11.1 hours (-$1,332.00) to 170.5 hours and legal assistant fees will be reduced by 1.3 hours (-$78.00) to 233.3 hours.

Next, a cursory review of Exhibit R in applicant's EAJA application reveals a total of 17.6 billable hours - 36.8 of which were expended on researching the legislative history of the EAJA and the definition of administrative adjudication. Fees of this type, solely for the purpose of educating counsel, are not recoverable from the agency under the EAJA. Accordingly, the billable hours for applicant's law clerk fees will be reduced by 36.7 hours (-$1512.00) to .8 hours.

A review of the itemized statement of time reflects that this applicant is entitled to attorney fees in the amount of $34, 530.00 (that is, 170.5 hour @ $120 per hour, 233.3 hours @ $60 per hour, and .8 hours at $90.00). Accordingly, the EAJA awards and the Administrator must pay this applicant $34,530 in attorney's fees.

The applicant has also filed for an additional $5,780.56 covering a list of miscellaneous expense. Expenses of this type (photocopying, postage, long distance telephone charges, supplies, travel, etc.) incurred by the applicant are recoverable by the EAJA. Rooney v. Administrator 5 NTSB 776, 777-778. However, a review of the list provides no specificity for a number of expenses incurred. For example, there are lump totals for long distance telephone calls and faxes ($798.73), postage ($308 .48), courier service ($25.00), photocopying ($233.75), Westlaw legal research ($227.00) and supplies ($52.54). Yet, there are neither explanations nor receipts to account for such expenditures. Such lack of specificity provides no means of determining when and where such expenses were incurred and whether they were related to this matter. The Board has previously held that when the application for attorney's fees lacks specificity and documentation, the law judge can deny these claims that are not supported adequately. More v. Administrator Order EAJA-2169 Page 3, Note 5. That being the case, the applicant is not entitled to recover the expenses of those telephone calls and faxing, postage, courier service, photocopying, Westlaw legal research, and supplies which lack specificity and documentation, all in the amount $1,535.10.

On a similar note, the Board has previously held that while "award for round trip air fare, (hotel and meals) of the applicant's attorney is an expense contemplated by the EAJA, the travel expense for the applicant for air fare (hotels and parking) from his residence to the hearing site is not an expense contemplated by the EAJA". Rooney at 777. Therefore, the applicant is not entitled to his airfare of $294.00 or his mileage of $329.67 ($130.65 and $199.02), and the expenses will be reduced by this total of $565.67. Since this applicant has provided only lump sums for hotel rooms ($1,158.24) and meals ($331.64), for client, attorney, legal assistant, and witnesses, such totals will be reduced by 25% ($289.56 and $82.76) for a total of $372.32.

Accordingly, the amount requested for "expenses" shall be adjusted to $3307.47.

## ORDER

It is therefore ORDERED AND DECREED that the applicant herein be awarded fees and expenses under the Equal Access to Justice Act in the amount of $37,837.47.

AND IT IS SO ORDERED.

Entered and served on this 13th Day of February 1998, at Arlington, Texas

Honorable William R. Mullins
Administrative Law Judge

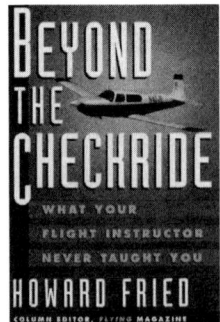

# The GPS
# Resource Guide

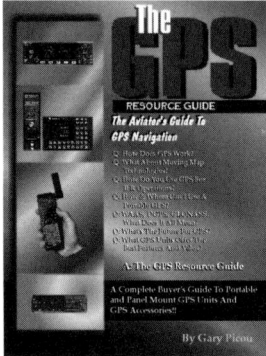

GPS is undoubtedly the best way to "Show Me The Way To Go Home!"... and now Kindred Spirit Press shows you far more than the way home. This book explains *everything* you ever wanted to know about a navigation system that has single-handedly revolutionized the aviation world! This ultimate aero-consumer guidebook to GPS aviation navigation is written by a true expert in the field. It features a comprehensive Buyer's Guide, easy to understand tips on GPS purchase and operation, and real answers to your most important questions on GPS navigation!

**Publication Date: Late 1999... Order NOW for $29.95 and get FREE shipping to your home the minute it comes off press! Soft-cover, 200+ pages, ISBN: 1-886743-16-9**

# The SportPlane
# Resource Guide...
# Second Edition!!!

Finally... Jim Campbell (and a cast of thousands... or so it seems) has re-edited and rewritten the much celebrated SportPlane Resource Guide... adding nearly 400 pages, 200 new aircraft, dozens of extraordinary "How-To" chapters and updated everything in sight! This book offers 1100 pages of ultralights, rotorcraft, powered parachutes, affordable flyers, high performance homebuilts, hot-air balloons, you name it! It has NO equal!

NO other book has as much expert and objective information on TODAY's SportPlanes. NO other book has as much industry expertise within its covers. NO other book has tackled the best and worst of the SportPlane industry and "Told It Like It Is" the way that Campbell has... and he's done it yet again!

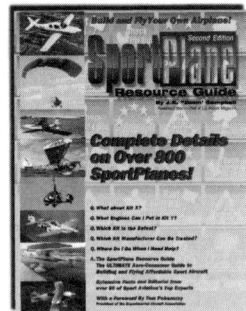

**Order your copy now! Immediate shipping! ISBN 1-886743-14-2, 1100 pages, $39.95**

Fax orders: (941) 294-3678. Please send this form with order.

Telephone orders: Call 1 (800) 356-7767 toll free, (941)294-6396. (Please have your credit card ready).

E-Mail: Publisher@kindredspirit.com
http://www.kindredspirit.com

Postal orders: Mail To: Aero-Media USA, Inc., P.O. Box 9132, Winter Haven, FL 33883-9132

Please send the following Books. I understand that I may return any of them for a full refund–for any reason, no questions asked.

_____

_____

_____

## Please send me more FREE information on:
❑ Other books, ❑ Speaking/Seminars, ❑ Consulting

Name:_____

Address:_____

City:_____State: _____Zip: _____ — ____

Telephone:_____

E-mail address:_____

**\*Shipping SPRG- $5.50 (US), $10 (Foreign)**
**\*\*Shipping All Other Books- $3.50 (US), $5 (Foreign)**

**Payment: ❑Check, ❑Money Order,**
**❑Credit Card: ❑Visa ❑MasterCard ❑AmEx**

Card Number:_____

Name on card:_____ Exp. date: ____/____